Trade Agreements
and
Financial Services

Trade Agreements
and
Financial Services

Hazel J Johnson
University of Louisville, Kentucky, USA

Patricia M Langley
University of Louisville, Kentucky, USA

World Scientific
New Jersey • London • Singapore • Hong Kong

332
J67t

Published by

World Scientific Publishing Co. Pte. Ltd.
5 Toh Tuck Link, Singapore 596224
USA office: Suite 202, 1060 Main Street, River Edge, NJ 07661
UK office: 57 Shelton Street, Covent Garden, London WC2H 9HE

British Library Cataloguing-in-Publication Data
A catalogue record for this book is available from the British Library.

TRADE AGREEMENTS AND FINANCIAL SERVICES

ISBN 981-02-4248-4
ISBN 981-02-4249-2 (pbk)

This book is printed on acid-free paper.

Printed in Singapore by Mainland Press

In Loving Memory of

Ida W. Kelly and Lucille V. Johnson,

whose love and dedication

will always shine brightly in my heart and mind.

H. J. Johnson

For My Mother,

Frances P. Langley,

"The future is always changing.

We create the future:

with our words, our deeds and with our beliefs."

P. M. Langley

Preface

When the North American Free Trade Agreement (NAFTA) was debated prior to its enactment, the focus was on the manufacturing sector and the jobs that would be lost to Mexico. The fear was that the United States would become a hollowed-out shell of its former self — with some compelling examples of U.S. firms moving jobs to Mexico in support of the arguments against NAFTA. Neither the outspoken legislators nor the media covering the treaty-approval process commented on the most profound aspects of NAFTA — the multilateral agreement on investments in the financial services sector. For the first time in the Western Hemisphere, foreign investments in banks, securities firms, and the insurance sector would be governed by mutually agreed upon rules of conduct and dispute resolution.

A well-functioning financial services sector is critical to economic development. In a market economy, it is through these markets and institutions that economic development is facilitated. Capital is mobilized and invested in the private sector — businesses that create jobs, increase productivity, and support the growth of a middle class. As the middle class grows, savings increase. These savings can then be invested directly into the business sector (stocks and bonds) or into financial institutions (for example, banks, insurance companies, or mutual funds) that invest in the business sector. A well-functioning financial sector is the *sine qua non* of economic development — without it, there will be no development.

As technological advances continue to be made, the ease of cross-border financial services grows — almost exponentially. Information can be sent and received within seconds. Data can be stored and transported on small credit-card-size devices. Access to information — anything from individual account data to large public or proprietary data bases — is possible from a desktop computer, a laptop computer, or a telephone. The delivery of financial services has been revolutionized as a result of these advances.

Trade agreements in Asia, Latin America, and Europe all acknowledge the importance of the financial services sector — a critical element of economic development.

About the Authors

Hazel J. Johnson is Distinguished University Scholar and Professor of Finance at the University of Louisville (Kentucky, USA). She has authored more than 25 books in the areas of international banking, bank asset/liability management, bank valuation, corporate finance and international economics, and her work has been translated into Chinese, Japanese, and Spanish. In addition, she has developed software systems for business practitioners in the areas of bank valuation, capital budgeting, cost of capital, and mergers and acquisitions. Dr. Johnson has taught at Georgetown University, Washington, D.C., and has acted as a consultant to more than 50 major U.S. banks and a number of state and federal agencies.

Patricia M. Langley is an adjunct professor in the College of Business and Public Administration of the University of Louisville (Kentucky, USA). She holds the degree of Master of Science in Library and Information Science. Ms. Langley also serves as reference librarian and business library liaison officer for Spalding University in Louisville while completing the degree of Master of Business Administration.

About the Authors

Contents

Chapter 1

Trade Agreements and Their Critical Elements

Introduction

If there was but one lesson learned in the wake of World War II, it was the interdependence of every country's economic and financial stability upon the stability of all others. No country could exist, economically speaking, as an island. This lesson was felt strongly as industrialized nations scrambled to rebuild what was left of their economies and financial infrastructures and move back into a non-wartime mode of operation (Bergsten 2001). In attempts to help one's own country by reaching out to other countries, several new multilateral institutions formed — dedicated to increased international economic cooperation. Among the most notable of these institutions are those that were born out of the Bretton Woods Accords — the World Bank and the International Monetary Fund.

The provisions of the General Agreement on Tariffs and Trade (GATT) are points of reference for virtually every trade agreement in force or in negotiation. In this way, GATT sets the worldwide standards for managing tariff and non-tariff barriers to international trade. In so doing, GATT also sets the foundation for international trade in financial services.

GATT: The Foundations for All Trade Agreements

The **General Agreement on Tariffs and Trade**, signed at the Geneva Trade Conference in 1947 by representatives of twenty-three non-Communist nations, including the United States, was the culmination of efforts beginning in 1946. At that time, there was provisional acceptance of a charter to create an international forum dedicated to (1) the expansion of multilateral trade and (2) the conciliation and settlement of international trade disputes. These original twenty-three countries were among many which originally agreed to a draft Charter for an International Trade Organization (ITO) as a new agency under the United Nations. This early effort was intended to boost trade liberalization after the Second World War and to begin correcting pre-War-era policies of protectionism through tariff negotiations. The first round of negotiations resulted in 45,000 tariff concessions affecting $10 billion in world trade. These tariff concessions and rules together became known as the General Agreement on Tariffs and Trade and became effective in January 1948. They were intended to provide not only world trade disciplines but also contained rules relating to employment, commodity agreements, restrictive business practices, international investment and services.

In the intervening years, the treaty has been accepted by many more nations bringing the total to 111 nations adhering to GATT as full contracting parties, another 22 countries and territories participating under various arrangements, including de facto treaty acceptance by 1993. Although trade negotiations are ongoing in nature, since 1947 GATT members have sponsored many specially organized rounds of negotiations as part of the on-going process. These rounds have continued to examine trade and tariff agreements in various areas to continue reducing barriers as new members become involved in the efforts and work to GATT compliance.

The Motivation for GATT

In the nineteenth century, international trade was governed by two basic principles:

- The greater the economic differences between two countries, the greater their propensity to trade.
- The benefits of such trade are maximized under conditions of free trade.

In a sense, two countries with different economies could complement each other in a free trade environment. The two assumptions under which free trade yielded the greatest benefits were:

- Market imperfections, such as monopolies or restrictive tariffs, did not exist.

- No country could possibly improve its access to other markets by restricting its own imports from these markets.

The United Kingdom was the pioneer of free trade principles in 1846 when it unilaterally abolished its restrictions on the trading of corn. By the 1870s, this philosophy had resulted in the formation of a multitude of bilateral trade agreements in Europe. Each of these pacts had a common feature — the unconditional **most-favored-nation (MFN) clause**.

This clause stipulated that each of the two countries in a bilateral agreement must offer the other any trade privilege that it granted to a third party. Because there were so many bilateral agreements in Europe, effectively they created a multilateral trade agreement. Under this system of liberalization, cross-border trade expanded rapidly.

However, this 19th-century spirit of trade liberalization was severely dampened by the protectionist legislation and practices that followed the Stock Market Crash of 1929. During the depression years of 1929 to 1932, the volume of world output declined by 20% and the volume of world trade fell at the even faster rate of 40%. The framers of GATT sought to reverse these effects (Abu-Akeel 1999).

The Basic Principles

During and after World War II (1939–1945), the British and the Americans led the initiative to restore to the world trade arena the principles of **comparative advantage**, **multilateralism**, and **nondiscrimination** (http://www.wto.org/).

- The theory of **comparative advantage** suggests that nations should (1) export those products that they can produce more efficiently than other nations and (2) import those products for which they are relative high-cost producers.
- **Multilateralism** is a policy that seeks to permit international trade without restrictive bilateral arrangements that may prevent trading partners from fully realizing their comparative advantage. That is, bilateral trade agreements should not discourage trade with other, third party countries.
- **Nondiscrimination** prevents nations from applying treatment to either imports or exports that favors one nation at the expense of another.

On January 1, 1948, GATTwas signed by over 80 fully participating countries and by almost 30 that signed special arrangements. GATT addressed reciprocal commercial rights and spelled out obligations of the signatories, explicitly including the concept of MFN treatment. Through GATT, common regulations and a framework for negotiating trade-liberalizing agreements were established.

GATT member countries assess trade policies and propose new policies in an effort to minimize new or existing trade barriers. This is accomplished in two ways: by reducing import tariffs and quotas or by abolishing preferential trade agreements between member countries. To reduce import tariff barriers, tariff concessions are negotiated on the principle of reciprocity. Once a concession is made on an item, then the concession reciprocally applies to all contracting parties. Thus, an item is bound against higher tariffs. As an economic safety measure, a country can request to withdraw its original concession, via an escape clause, should a tariff reduction cause serious injury to its domestic industry. To abolish preferential trade agreements, member countries recognize a principle of nondiscriminatory trade relations between all member countries. This is accomplished through a policy of most-favored-nation status among members. All tariffs, whether or not determined by a concession, are included under this policy. This principle of equality also governs GATT members' efforts to abolish of all non-tariff barriers to trade.

Because of GATT, since the end of World War II, world trade has expanded faster than world output. The average worldwide tariff declined from 40% in 1947 to approximately 5% in the mid-1990s. "Rounds" of trade talks have facilitated this process. For example:

- During the **Dillon Round** (1960–1962), the Common External Tariff was adopted in which the United States granted concessions for agricultural exports by other countries.
- The **Kennedy Round** (1964–1967) reduced tariffs by 35% to 40%, improved access to worldwide agricultural markets, and expanded the outlets for exports of less developed countries.
- The **Tokyo Round** (1973–1979) concentrated on a new set of tariff cuts and reducing other barriers to trade. The negotiators worked on a GATT Codes of Conduct, that is, an instrument that prescribes the standards of behavior by nations and govern the use of non-tariff barriers to trade. Only signatories to each code are bound by its

terms.[1] One of these codes of conduct involved government purchases, granting favored status to developing countries without seeking reciprocal arrangements. Another was the GATT Customs Valuation Code, that is, a formula (agreed to multilaterally) for appraising imported items for the purpose of setting the amount of duty payable by the importer in the importing country.

The Uruguay Round

The most recent round, the **Uruguay Round** (1986–1994) was the most difficult to conclude. From the outset, there was an ambitious agenda that broached the most sensitive issues involving the trade of goods and services.

From the outset, an ambitious agenda broached the most sensitive issues involving the trade of goods and services. In December 1990, the talks broke off when the United States and the European Community (now the European Union) remained deadlocked on the issue of EU farm subsidies. Altogether, there were unresolved matters in 15 broad areas including farming, patents, financial services, telecommunications, and textiles.

The **Montreal Round** was actually a meeting in December of 1988 among 96 nations for the purpose of expressing political urgency for successful conclusion of the Uruguay Round that had began in 1986. This meeting resulted in an agreement to:

- Liberalize trade in services.
- More swiftly settle trade disputes.
- Allow freer trade in tropical products, such as coffee, rubber, and bananas.
- Reduce tariffs by 30%.
- Ease non-tariff barriers.
- Ease investment restrictions.
- Monitor an individual country's trade policies.

There were four areas in which the attendees of the meeting could not agree:

- Liberalizing trade in agriculture.
- Instituting protections for intellectual property.

---

[1] The phrase GATT Code of Conduct is synonymous with Multinational Trade Negotiations Code, or MTN Code.

- Implementing textile trade reforms.
- Establishing rules for protection against imports.

Early in 1994, the Uruguay Round was completed, including the resolution of some of the most difficult issues and the creation of a new trade organization. The World Trade Organization (WTO) began in 1997. This international group rules on trade disputes between signatories of GATT. Critics of the new GATT cite the potential loss of national sovereignty that the WTO represents, the loss of government revenues from tariffs, and the loss of jobs from competition from imports. However, proponents of the new GATT point to the benefits of the arrangement:

- The reduction of tariff and non-tariff barriers that can increase worldwide output by more than $5 trillion (U.S. output by more than $1 trillion) over 10 years.
- The protection of intellectual property rights (patents and copyrights), which could prevent the loss from piracy and counterfeiting of an estimated $60 billion per year by U.S. businesses.
- New market opportunities for U.S. services firms, which export $163 billion per year, as international services trade is liberalized.
- Removal of significant barriers to overseas investment.
- Fair competition and open markets in agriculture, especially for U.S. farmers who lead the world in agricultural exports at $40 billion per year.
- Full participation of developing countries in global trade, which could significantly increase U.S. exports by as much as $200 billion over the next 10 years.
- Strengthened rules for dispute settlement that should reduce the uncertainty of foreign market participation and provide fairer competition from foreign competitors in the home market.

The Final Act of the Uruguay Round contained a number of agreements, including agreements on agriculture, intellectual property, textiles, and import licensing procedures (Zekos 1999).

Also, among the issues addressed in the Final Act of the Uruguay Round was a General Agreement on Trade in Services (Services Agreement). The Services Agreement is composed of three parts:

- The **Framework Agreement** contains the basic obligations that apply to all member countries.

- **National schedules** contain specific commitments by individual countries to continue to liberalize the services sectors of their economies.
- The **annexes** address special situations of the services sectors.

The Services Agreement covers a broad range of activities in which services are supplied from the territory of one party (member country) to the territory of another party:
- Services supplied in the territory of one party to the consumers of any other (for example, tourism)
- Services provided by nationals of one party in the territory of any other (for example, construction projects or consulting)
- Services provided through the presence of service-providing entities of one party in the territory of another (for example, banking)

In all of these situations, each member country must "accord immediately and unconditionally to services and service providers of any other Party, treatment no less favorable than that it accords to like services and service providers of any other country."[2] That is, member countries must accord MFN status in services as well as merchandise trade. In those cases in which MFN status is not possible, that is, when MFN exemptions exist, such exceptions must be specified in an annex and the annex must indicate the specific MFN exemption that is relevant. However, these exemptions must be reviewed after five years and normally may not exceed 10 years in duration.

In addition, the national schedules of individual member countries contain commitments for **market access** and **national treatment**. With respect to foreign service providers, market access provisions eliminate limitations on:
- Numbers of service providers
- Total value of service transactions
- Total number of service operations
- Total number of people employed
- Foreign investment
- Level of foreign participation

---

[2] "General Agreement on Trade in Services," A Summary of the Final Act of the Uruguay Round, http://www.wto.org

National treatment provisions require a member country to treat service providers of other countries in the same way in which domestic service providers are treated. That is, the conditions of competition cannot be modified to favor domestic service providers.

One of the annexes addresses financial services, primarily banking and insurance. Member countries are entitled to take prudential measures, that is, to regulate financial services, for the protection of investors, bank deposit holders, and insurance policy holders. The annex also recognizes the need to maintain the integrity and stability of the financial system. With respect to **market access**, the annex addresses the responsibility of each member country not to impede insurance policy writing, financial data processing, financial data transfer, establishment or expansion of a commercial presence, and the temporary entry of personnel. In terms of **national treatment**, the annex specifies that there must be access to payments and clearing systems operated by public entities (such as the Federal Reserve System) and to official funding and refinancing facilities (such as the sale of U.S. Treasury securities). National treatment must also be accorded in the areas of membership, or participation, in self-regulatory bodies (such as the U.S. National Association of Securities Dealers), securities exchanges (such as the New York Stock Exchange), futures exchanges (such as the Chicago Mercantile Exchange), and clearing agencies (such as the Federal Reserve System).

The World Trade Organization

The **World Trade Organization** (WTO) is a single institutional framework that encompasses the GATT, as modified by the Uruguay Round, all GATT agreements and all GATT arrangements.

The objective of the WTO is to help its members conduct their trade and economic relations in order to:
• Raise standards of living
• Ensure full employment
• Steadily increase incomes and demand for goods and services
• Expand production and trade in goods and services
  Functionally, the WTO:
• Administers and implements multilateral trade agreements
• Acts as a forum for multilateral trade negotiations
• Seeks to resolve trade disputes

- Oversees national trade policies
- Cooperates with other international institutions (such as the International Monetary Fund and the World Bank) that are involved in economic policy-making

Based in Geneva, Switzerland, the WTO is governed through Ministerial Conference meetings that occur at least once every two years. The General Council oversees implementation of the agreements and ministerial decisions. The General Council is also a Dispute Settlement Body and a Trade Policy Review Mechanism. The General Council delegates responsibilities to three other bodies:
- Council for Trade in Goods
- Council for Trade in Services
- Council for Trade-Related Aspects of Intellectual Property Rights

By 1997, 131 governments were members of the WTO. By 2002, the number had grown to 143. But, unlike GATT, which was a multilateral agreement organizing itself under the power the United Nations, the World Trade Organization is a separate, permanent institution with its own secretariat. GATT was still only applied on a "provisional basis" even after more than fifty-five years. The WTO commitments are full and permanent. The GATT rules applied to trade in merchandise goods. In addition to goods, the WTO covers trade in services and trade-related aspects of intellectual property. While GATT was a multilateral instrument, by the 1980s many new agreements had been added of a plurilateral, or selective, nature. The agreements that constitute the WTO are multilateral and require commitment from the entire membership. The WTO dispute settlement system is faster, more automatic, and thus much less susceptible to blockages, than the old GATT system. The implementation of WTO dispute findings will also be more easily assured. While the WTO to some extent replaces it, GATT lives on as "GATT 1994", the amended and up-dated version of GATT from 1947, which is an integral part of the WTO Agreement and which continues to provide the key disciplines affecting international trade in goods (Ahn 2000).

Regional Trade Agreements Under GATT and WTO

Article XXIV of GATT allows the development of regional trade pacts by acknowledging the desirability of enhancing trade freedoms through the development of voluntary arrangements for the closer coordination of specific economies. However, in keeping with the basic principles of free trade, Article XXIV stipulates three conditions for such arrangements:

- Duties, tariffs, and other restrictions with respect to trade between the parties to the trade agreement must not be higher than before the agreement.

- Duties and other restrictive regulations must be eliminated on substantially all the trade between the parties to the agreement.

- Interim agreements must lead to a final, permanent arrangement within a reasonable length of time.

Over time, and especially during the Uruguay Round of GATT, there has been some frustration with operating solely under the provisions of GATT. For example, GATT permits preferential treatment for developing countries. However, as the developing countries have become "newly industrializing," there has been pressure on some of them to more fully adopt the free-trade principles of GATT and now the WTO. Also, some trade issues, such as intellectual property rights, have been difficult to manage under GATT and the WTO. Finally, geographical proximities of countries to neighboring nations sometimes make it more efficient to address specific issues through bilateral or regional agreements. Thus, there has been a growing tendency for regional trade agreements.

The WTO now maintains the primacy, or priority, of the multilateral trading system. At the same time, the WTO established a new Committee on Regional Trade Agreements to coordinate the processes of global and regional trade liberalization. The committee reviews the legality of regional trade agreements and reports back to the World Trade Organization on any aspects of regional trade agreements that undermine the multilateral trading system so that sanctions may be taken if necessary. Though there has been some study as to whether regionalism promoted by such trade agreements undermines multilateralism, no clear conclusions have been made (Levy 93). However, regional trade agreements do appear to give greater bargaining position to those countries with weaker or smaller economies when paired with more healthier or larger ones.

The Stages of Regional Integration

Regional integration into trading partnerships achieves one goal. Regional integration removes artificial barriers to trade and allows the market itself play a central role in harmonizing member countries economic policies. Protectionism has been a long-standing tradition for many countries. Easing certain restrictions on trade is difficult for many countries. Yet, there are many reasons for the formation of regional trading blocs. Simple geographical proximity and the perceived added value of working towards common in economic, cultural, and social interests, not withstanding the possibility of allaying fears of potential conflicts, is a factor in the decision to enter into trade alliances. Geographical proximity political and ideological aspects can also be a motivating factor. Not to be excluded, however, is the cost benefit analysis approach. If the benefits outweigh the costs, then a country is not motivated to join and reap the benefits. Protectionism doesn't necessarily pay (Blount 1999).

The process of regional integration has been classified in five stages.[3] Each successive stage implies closer economic integration between the member countries than the preceding stage.

- Free Trade Area
- Customs Union
- Common Market
- Economic Union
- Complete Economic Integration

In a **free trade area**, tariffs and quantitative restrictions between the member countries are eliminated. However, trade policy of each member country vis-à-vis countries outside the free trade area is left to the discretion of each member country. A **customs union** is a free trade area in which the member countries also jointly determine the level of tariffs on goods from outside the free trade area. In a **common market**, not only tariffs and duties on goods are eliminated, but also factors of production (labor and capital) may flow freely between the member countries. When countries are part of an **economic union**, the common market member countries coordinate national economic policies (to a greater or lesser extent). When there is **complete economic integration** between the member countries, national

---

[3] These stages were developed by Bela Balassa and are the most frequently cited. (See Goto, Irie, and Soyama, The Current Situation and Prospects for Regional Economic Integration.)

economic policies are completely coordinated. The member countries virtually become one new country with the formation of supranational entities and a single monetary system.

Countries undertaking any sort of trade union typically progress through this process along a predictable course from free trade area, through customs union, to common market to economic union to a political union. Currently, this process or model is being used extensively as the method of bringing more countries into the European Union. Furthermore, it is a model for economic integration widely used among developing countries. However, in many cases this approach turned out to be misleading, because these states did not take into consideration the pre-conditions necessary for successful economic integration (e.g., their unique economic and political systems and historical differences).

In other words, successful integration processes need time and patience. Primarily, it is necessary to direct states' efforts toward cooperation on concrete projects, in order to establish the pre-conditions for further integration of separate economies or as the basis for greater goals. It is difficult to draw a line of division between the economic and political aspects of regional integration. The main characteristic of "new regionalism" is that it is multifaceted. Extensive political and security goals are achieved through economic integration. Moreover, even if regionalism is based upon economic goals, it is unlikely to prove an existence of serious differences (divergences) in other questions (fields).

In Wilfred J. Ethier's analysis of the "**new regionalism**," several characteristics are presented that might give some insight for why there has been a rash of regional trading blocs since the 1980s. Ethier has found that smaller, less economically well-placed countries tend to pair up with larger ones creating a dominant partner in each new trading block. Ethier cites the United States for NAFTA and Brazil for Mercosur.

Very typically, the smaller countries involved in these blocs have recently made or are in the process of making radical or "significant unilateral reforms" in at least some area of government, trade, or finance. Moving away from communism, for many central European countries has been this radical move.

In Ethier's model, many of these regional trade agreements address much more than only trade barriers. This new regionalism is taking place in a context of wide economic and even social reform. The degree of trade liberalization still tends to be rather low and is typically more unilateral than multilateral. The liberalization that is achieved is due to concessions by the small countries in most circumstances (Ethier 2001).

Financial Services under the North American Free Trade Agreement (NAFTA)

Signed January 1, 1994, the North American Free Trade Agreement resulted in a continent-wide free trade zone encompassing the United States, Canada, and Mexico to be fully implemented over a 10-year period. Either duty-free access or reduced duty access was arranged for thousands of items. Provisions designed to make customs administration easier and to help solve disputes on customs matters quicker were also implemented.

NAFTA also created the most extensive and powerful set of protections of any multinational agreement for investors of all NAFTA member countries in the territory of any other NAFTA member country including an international arbitration tribunal for compensation of losses. Services are the greatest vehicle of growth in the economies of all three member countries (Abbott 2000). NAFTA provides a strong infrastructure of rights for international service users and providers across a broad-spectrum sub industry in this area.

The Financial Services Chapter of the North America Free Trade Agreement (Chapter 14) outlines the treatment that each government involved in the agreement must afford financial institutions or services from the other two countries. Chapter 14 delineates the principles and protections governing for opening the participants' financial sectors to the supply of services through either cross-border trade or the local establishment by outside financial suppliers without interfering with national approaches to financial sector regulation. Chapter 14 includes two separate elements. The first is the framework agreed upon by the three countries and the second are the annexes specific reservations to the agreement that are declared by each country.

Under NAFTA, the financial services that are provided within the United States, Canada, and Mexico (the three Parties) must conform to certain standards of treatment and disclosure. Generally speaking, establishment of financial institutions within the territory of one Party by investors that reside in the territory of another Party is permitted within certain guidelines, subject to review by the three Parties. Disputes are to be settled according to predetermined procedure and any expropriation of investments must be fairly compensated.

Establishment of Financial Institutions

Article 1403 of NAFTA governs the establishment of financial services under this trade agreement. Through this agreement, each country recognizes that investors from one country are permitted to establish financial institutions in another country's territory under the jurisdiction chosen by the investor and participate in that country's financial market. Participation is defined as the ability to provide financial services, to expand geographically, and to own financial institutions without being subject to ownership requirements specific to foreign financial institutions.

Each Party must be permitted to engage in a wide range of financial services. In fact, the section that refers to establishment of financial institutions states that a financial institution must be permitted to expand geographically and not be held accountable to the normal ownership requirements for foreign financial institutions. Each Party may prohibit **direct branching** into its territory, but a financial institution that resides in one Party must be permitted to establish a presence in the territory of the other two Parties via a subsidiary.

Originally, direct branching into Mexico and Canada was prohibited because U.S. federal law did not permit nationwide branching. However, there is a specific provision that, at such time as the United States does permit commercial banks of another Party to expand either through subsidiaries or direct branches throughout the United States, then both Mexico and Canada will review this policy and perhaps relax this particular aspect of the agreement. This part of the agreement was viewed as an incentive for the United States to review its own policies with respect to nationwide branching.[4]

Each Party (that acts as a host country for the financial institution of another Party) may require the investors of the other Party to incorporate under the host country law. The host country also has the right to impose on foreign institutions the same sorts of restrictions and regulations that it imposes on indigenous institutions.

---

[4] The Riegle-Neal Act permitted nation wide branching in the United States beginning in 1997.

Cross Border Trade

According to the principles delineated in Chapter 14, NAFTA countries must allow their residents to acquire financial services from providers located in other NAFTA territories. No new restrictions can be imposed on cross-border financial services with the exception of any reservations that a country may have made in the specific section in the NAFTA Annex set aside for that purpose.

Cross-border trade is defined as the transactions by which financial suppliers supply their services from their home country to customers in another country. Freedom of cross-border trade implies the absence of obstacles to the trade in goods and services. Cross-border trade is recognized, defined, and outlined in Article 1404, which prohibits any of the three countries from adopting measures that restrict cross-border trade in financial services by cross-border financial service providers of another country except under certain conditions set out in the agreement. This means that no new measures restricting cross border trade can be established. Current measures may still stand until dealt with as the member countries consult further to create free market access.

The United States, Canada and Mexico have agreed formally not to restrict cross-border trade in the provision of financial services. The history of this provision is linked primarily to the nationalization of Mexican Banks in 1982, the beginning of the so-called Latin American debt crisis. At the same time that banks were nationalized, Mexican citizens were prohibited from buying financial services from financial institutions in other countries. This was done in effect to stem the flight of investment capital from Mexico. NAFTA specifically states that it will no longer be permissible for one of the three Parties to impose such restrictions.

Explicitly, no Party may adopt any measure that would restrict the free flow of financial services. Each Party must allow its own citizens to purchase financial services from cross-border financial service providers that reside either in the territory of the Party or in the territory of any other Party to the agreement. Under this provision, a U.S. financial services provider may now sell financial services to Mexican citizens whether it has an operation in Mexico, United States, or Canada. As is true in many other facets of the agreement, each Party may require a cross-border provider of financial services to register with the respective Party in the normal course of business.

One remaining obstacle is lack of tax harmonization and the ability to use specific taxation measures to stem the flow of financial services across the borders. A second is remaining limitation rules in one country that might restrict the ability of foreign suppliers to meet domestic demands for services.

National Treatment

Language that became critical in negotiations of the European Union with respect to financial services now appears in NAFTA. The concept of national treatment has been incorporated as one of the cornerstones of the agreement. **National treatment** means that each Party must accord treatment that is no less favorable than that it accords its own financial service institutions, investments, or investors. The objective is to ensure that no excessively burdensome regulations placed on financial institutions of one Party when they establish a presence in another Party. The standard is applied to all facets of operation including establishment, acquisition, expansion, management, conduct, operation and sale, or other disposition of financial institutions and investments. This is a binding obligation of each Party whether the institution is operating within the national boundaries of the Party or whether the institution is providing cross-border financial services. In addition, each federal government is obligated to ensure that no state or province imposes regulations that would violate the national treatment standard.

It should be noted that national treatment requires treatment that is no less favorable than that of indigenous institutions. However, in no way does this imply a competitive advantage to the foreign institution. Instead, the foreign institution will not be subjected to competitive disadvantage. Furthermore, nothing in the national treatment obligations requires specific outcomes. In other words, there are no guarantees with respect to size or profitability or any other outcomes of doing business. National treatment provides the opportunity, not the guarantee, of access to the markets of other Parties.

National treatment, as outlined in Article 1405, requires the extension to imported goods and services of treatment no less favorable than that accorded to domestic goods and services with respect to internal taxes, laws, regulations, and requirements. NAFTA members are obliged to accord to one another national treatment with respect to internal measures that can affect trade. Foreign investors must be treated at least as well as local ones. This means that both formal and substantive rules cannot be structured to give an advantage to local companies. Allowing foreign firms establishment alone does not assure that foreign firms are free to serve another country's needs for financial services. The domestic firm must allow them the opportunity to perform their services.

There are two possible approaches to national treatment: **de jure national treatment** and **competitive national treatment**. De jure national treatment treats all companies as equal under the law whereas the competitive treatment allows for some flexibility in the application of the law so that foreign institutions are not placed at a disadvantage simply for not being a domestic company. NAFTA tends more toward the competitive national treatment in that NAFTA defines national treatment as "treatment no less favorable than that accorded by a party" the condition of "equal competitive opportunities," still applies to foreign suppliers (Abu-Keel 1999). The main goal is to provide the opportunity to provide, not to guarantee the success of the venture.

To further encourage individual states and provinces to market themselves to foreign firms, these foreign firms can request to be treated no less favorably than the best treatment they receive any other state or province of that country. In the case, of all three countries in NAFTA, individual states and provinces have some level of local autonomy that can lead to some confusion over the application of these regulations. This provision makes for a spirit more conducive toward inviting outside investment.

Most Favored Nation Treatment

Article 1406 defines the Most-Favored Nation Treatment accepted among the member countries of NAFTA. While this provision of NAFTA may sound somewhat like a reiteration of the previous, this provision applies to how NAFTA members treat each other over non -member nations. Essentially, no member of NAFTA will provide preferential treatment to investors of a non-member country over a member country. Treatment, however, can be equal if accorded unilaterally, achieved through harmonization or other means, or through agreement by all parties. This is called prudential measures. In essence, the best treatment given to non-NAFTA country investors must be given to NAFTA country investors.

NAFTA countries must provide basic international rights to investors such as following treaty obligations in good faith, providing due process and equitable treatment to investments (Abu-Akeel 1999).

New Financial Services and Data Processing

In regards to creating new financial services, each member of NAFTA affords each other members' institutions the right to create these services similar to ones it permits its own institutions to create. However, it may determine the form and require certain authorizations for the provision of service. NAFTA members also agree to allow fellow members to transfer data across borders for ordinary business data processing in electronic of other forms without interference as required.

Under New Financial Services and Data Processing, one Party may not prohibit the financial institution of another Party from fully participating in any sort of deregulation or expansion of powers that occurs. Each Party must allow the financial institutions of another Party to provide the same new products that are permitted to be offered by indigenous financial institutions. For example, if the United States permits commercial banks to offer a new type of product, Mexican and Canadian banks will be permitted to offer the same product. This provision essentially ensures that deregulation in each country will be accompanied by an upgrading in the competitive opportunities of the financial institutions of the other two Parties.

In addition, each Party must permit the transmission of necessary information cross-border so that the normal types of marketing, sales, and other record-keeping information can be maintained. The transmission of such data can have significant ramifications, particularly as financial service products themselves become increasingly oriented toward technology applications. It also means that certain economies of scale can be realized in setting up a marketing operation in one country, with all the record-keeping and back-office operations in another country. For example, it may be possible to establish a credit card operation that would be located in the United States with a primary customer base either in Canada or Mexico.

Senior Management and Boards of Directors

Article 1408 addresses the conflicts of interest that may arise when NAFTA members may attempt to influence the power structures within financial institutions by requiring membership by certain percentages of one nationality or another. This article simply states that a country cannot require that a foreign firm hire or retain on its board of directors, in senior management, or in essential personnel members of a particular nationality.

In many cases, restrictions in international trade are imposed with respect to the key personnel of a company or a financial institution. For example, in the United States the board of directors of an Edge Act bank (a nationally chartered bank that conducts international business) must be composed of U.S. citizens. Under NAFTA, such restrictions either do not exist or have been substantially reduced. No Party may insist that the senior management of a financial institution be of any particular nationality. For example, a U.S. bank may open a subsidiary in Mexico and hire senior managers of any nationality, as it deems appropriate. Notice that this provision is not limited to senior managers from the three countries that are signatories to NAFTA, i.e., any nationality is possible. Clearly, this provides total flexibility in assembling a team of qualified professionals.

Similarly, under NAFTA a Party may not require that more than a simple majority of the board of directors be composed of nationals of the Party or persons residing in the territory of the Party. For example, the board of directors for a subsidiary in Canada can include members that do not reside in Canada. This makes it possible for Mexican or U.S. citizens to members of the board of a Canadian financial service subsidiary.

Transparency

Transparency refers to the degree to which trade policies and practices, and the process by which they are established, are open and predictable. The ability of any financial services firm to run efficiently requires information on how and where to begin — clear, concise, timely, and correct information. Article 1411 on transparency guarantees each member country a certain measure of clarity in the application process. Each NAFTA member country must facilitate the process of applying for entry into the financial market by investors and firms of another country through dissemination of the policies and procedures of applying. It must also allow these firms and investor, "to the extent practicable," the opportunity to comment, in advance, on new regulations. Applicants are also guaranteed the right to know application status and receive a decision on their application to operate without undue delay (Bhagwati 1998).

Before any Party may introduce a regulatory measure that will affect the operation of financial institutions, the Party must advise the other Parties in sufficient time to permit them to comment on the proposed change. The requirement is that interested parties should be notified. However, this notification can be accomplished through official publication, other written form, or any other form.

Also, with respect to application for permission to establish a financial institution or to provide financial services, each Party must make available to all interested persons, the requirements of the regulatory authorities in this connection. Once an application has been completed, it is the responsibility of the regulators of each Party to make a decision about that application within 120 days. If a decision cannot be reached in 120 days, the applicant must be promptly notified of the reason for the delay and the regulators of the Party must attempt to reach a decision as quickly as possible. In the interim, the regulatory authorities of the Party are obligated, upon request, to inform the applicant of the status of the application. The general principle of transparency is intended to ease the process of entry into the financial services industry in each NAFTA country. It standardizes the circumstances, feedback, and time frame that a financial institution should expect when applying for permission to operate in any of the three countries.

It should be noted that the general principle of transparency does not require a Party to provide access to any information that is related to the financial affairs and accounts of individual customers, financial institutions, or cross-border financial service providers. Nor does the transparency principle require that a Party provide any confidential information, the disclosure of which would impede law enforcement, be contrary to the public interest, or prejudice any legitimate commercial interest of particular enterprises. Essentially, the transparency clause ensures a reasonable procedural framework that does not violate what might be considered in the United States the constitutional right of privacy.

This article does not require the member country to give or allow access to a firm's information from a member country related to the financial affairs and accounts of individual customers or any confidential information that might be contrary to the public good.

Financial Services Committee

The member countries of NAFTA elect members to a financial services committee whose office is to supervise the implementation of the articles outlines in Chapter 14 of NAFTA, consider issues brought before it, and participate as authoritative members in the dispute settlement procedures that is outlined in the next section. This committee meets at least once per year to assess the functioning of NAFTA and report the results to the Free Trade Commission created in Article 2001 part d.

Dispute Settlement

Possibly the most pressing issue for the parties involved in NAFTA is how to deal with possible disputes in how financial services are implemented and treated under the treaty. Dispute settlement in the arena of financial services is the purview of Article 1414. It outlines the who, what, where, how, and timeframe for settling disputes as they arise. To date, several cases have been brought up for settlement.

Chapter 14 Article 1414 on dispute settlement is an expansion of the dispute settlement procedures outlined in Chapter 20 of NAFTA. Each member country maintains a roster of individuals, appointed by consensus, willing to serve as panelists for a term of three years. As panelists, these individuals may also be reappointed at the end of their terms. As members of this roster, these panelists are expected to have expertise in the area of financial services law and practice. These panelists are also expected to meet the Chapter 20 qualifications as well. In a dispute regarding financial services, if all parties agree, then the panel reviewing the case shall be composed entirely of financial services roster members. Otherwise, Article 2010 prevails and the panelists to hear the dispute are chosen as outline there (Rogers 1993).

If upon hearing the dispute, the panel finds a measure implemented by one party to be inconsistent with the contractual obligations, then there are several retaliatory measures that may be taken. If the measure in question affects only the financial services sector, then the complaining member party may suspend benefits only in the financial services sector. If the measure in question affects the financial services sector and any other sector, then the complaining member country may suspend benefits in the financial sector such that the effect will be equivalent. Finally, if the panel finds that the measure does not affect the financial services sector, then the complaining member country may not suspend benefits in the financial services sector.

As with any agreement, disputes will arise, however carefully negotiated the terms may be. The financial services section of NAFTA follows closely the general provisions of Chapter 11 for dispute negotiation with some differences allowing for the unique nature of trade in financial services.

Consultations

As a precursor to conflict, member countries may request consultations with each other regarding any matter arising under NAFTA that affects the financial services section. In good faith, each member country is required to give the one requesting the consultation sympathetic consideration to the request. The consulting members then report the results of their consultations to the Financial Services Committee at its annual meeting. Regulatory authorities may be requested to participate in issues that may affect operations of financial institutions or cross-border financial service providers (Zekos 1999).

A Party may request that regulatory authorities of another Party participate in consultations under this Article regarding the other Party's measures of general application that may affect the operations of financial institutions or cross-border financial service providers in the requesting member country's territory. These regulatory authorities are also empowered to disseminate to the applicant firm accurate information about the regulatory process in their jurisdiction.

Investment Transfers

NAFTA also addresses the ability of each of the three countries to allow its companies to transfer investment funds across borders. There is a particular provision provided in the chapter on investments that speaks to this issue. Each Party must permit an investor to transfer freely and without delay cash flows that are related to the operation of a business (profits, dividends, interest, capital gains, etc.), sale or liquidation of an asset, loan transactions, and other payments.

The NAFTA agreement also forbids a Party to place restrictions on the destination of these transfers. For example, a transfer that is not made into another NAFTA country may not be penalized. Nor may one Party require that a facility or an investment that is transferred out of the host country be transferred into one of the other two Parties of NAFTA. However, nothing in this section of the agreement prohibits a host country from preventing a transfer when it is related to other matters as long as the treatment is equitable and does not discriminate against a financial institution or an investor of one of the NAFTA countries. Examples of situations in which there may be laws affecting transfers of payments and investment are:

- Bankruptcy, insolvency, or protection of creditors' rights
- Issuing, trading, or dealing in securities.
- Criminal or penal offenses
- Reports of transfers of currencies or other monetary instruments
- Ensuring the satisfaction of judgments in judicial proceedings

Expropriation and Compensation

Agreements between two or more countries typically aim to provide a predictable climate for investments in each other's territories by companies based in each of the countries. Such agreements thus cover inward and outward investment between the two countries party to the agreement. Typically, such agreements provide reciprocal assurances that foreign investments, in accordance with the host country's laws, regulations, and policies are guaranteed fair and equitable treatment, including full protection and security of the investment, non-discriminatory treatment in applicable regulation, right of transfer of funds, and rules on expropriation and dispute settlement (Price 1995).

Expropriation specifically refers to the act where governments deny some benefit of property to an individual. The NAFTA guarantees full, swift and fair compensation to be paid after any government action that constitutes an expropriation or any act that is similar to expropriation via Article 1110. No party in any of the member countries may directly or indirectly nationalize or expropriate an investment of an investor of another in its territory or take a measure tantamount to expropriation, except under a handful of circumstances.

These circumstances are outlines as being for a public purpose, on a non-discriminatory basis, in accordance with due process of law and on payment of compensation for the loss of the investment equal to the fair market value of investment. This compensation is also expected to be paid in a timely fashion.

Also, the previous owner of expropriated investment may not be forced to face unreasonable foreign exchange risks. If the currency in which compensation is paid devalues significantly between the time of determination of the fair market value and the actual payment of compensation, the previous owner of the investment must be compensated for this devaluation.

If the payment is made in a **G-7 currency**, the payment must include interest at a commercially reasonable rate for that currency from the date of appropriation.[5] Since the three countries in the NAFTA agreement are the United States, Canada, and Mexico, the two G-7 currencies that are most likely to be used are the U.S. dollar and the Canadian dollar. Should the payment be made in a **non-G-7 currency**, actual compensation may be no less than the equivalent amount of compensation that would have resulted if a G-7 currency had been used. This stipulation includes both the principal and interest involved.

Arbitration for Transfers and Expropriation

A claimant must wait at least six months but no more than three years before filing a claim with the Tribunal. This clock starts on the date "on which investor first acquired or should have first acquired knowledge of the alleged breach." The filing of a claim amounts to submission of a claim to the arbitration process. However, notice must be given at least 90 days before the claim is actually submitted. Such notice will specify the name and address of the disputing investor, the name and address of the enterprise as applicable, provisions of NAFTA that have been breached, issues and factual matters relating to the claim, the relief sought, and the approximate amount of damages claimed.

The matter is then reviewed by a Tribunal, which is established in the same way the tribunals for other financial services matters are established. One member is appointed by the claimant, a second by the Party against which the claim is brought, and one by mutual agreement of the two Parties. The third arbiter is considered to be the presiding arbiter. The Tribunal may

---

[5] The Group of Seven or G-7 countries are the United States, Canada, the United Kingdom, Germany, France, Italy, and Japan.

make a final award in the case of a dispute in the form of monetary damages including interest, restoration of property, or some combination of these. Each NAFTA Party must provide for enforcement of such final awards by the Tribunal. While the Party against whom the final award is made has the right of appeal (through other international channels), once the appeal process is complete, the procedures are structured so that each award will ultimately be satisfied.

The provisions of NAFTA with respect to financial services represent one general set of rules for each country that is involved in the agreement. These provisions represent negotiated policies and procedures through which each country receives some measure of benefit. However, the benefit is not the same for each country. Banks and other financial service providers in the United States, Canada, and Mexico will derive distinctly different advantages as a result of the North American Free Trade Agreement.

Advantages of NAFTA for Financial Services

Several beneficial changes have occurred a result of NAFTA's financial services provisions. These changes range from reduced restrictions to beneficial flows of services that have helped avert other problems that are likely to occur when each country is left to their own. The implementation of limits during the transition period as NAFTA takes effect also allow for protection of vulnerable markets especially in Mexico while still allowing for solid investment opportunities for all three countries.

United States and Canadian financial services benefit as reduced financial restrictions mandated by NAFTA open the Mexican financial market to their firms. Also service providers such as customs brokers and other jobs related to the distribution and transportation of goods across the border have flourished. More importantly, NAFTA reduces obstacles to direct investment into Mexico, but it also eliminates certain Mexican regulations that made direct investment the only way to sell in the domestic Mexican market. Now, producers who otherwise would have had to locate in Mexico to serve the Mexican market can now simply export from their own country.

NAFTA's service provisions also played an important role in Mexico's peso crisis in 1994. NAFTA helped to bring a quick resolution to the crisis, as Mexico fulfilled its commitments and implemented a rigorous adjustment program. As a result, international investor confidence recovered quickly, allowing Mexico to return to international capital markets within seven months, compared to seven years after Mexico's 1982 crisis (Hazera 2000).

As a result of NAFTA, Canadian financial institutions have more transparency and certainty regarding access to US and Mexican markets. The financial services sector is vital to the Canadian economy. Canadian financial institutions are highly competitive internationally, and have significant export interests in North America and Latin America. The financial services sector contributes over 5 percent of Canada's gross domestic product and directly employs more than 500,000 people. Improved business opportunities resulting from NAFTA lead to new export and job opportunities in Canada. Increased competition in the domestic market provides Canadian consumers with greater choice in products, improved quality of service, and lower prices (Sczudlo 1993).

In general, foreign investment in Mexican companies had been limited previously to 49% or less. New investment rules in 1989 did liberalize some of these restrictions making 100% foreign investment possible in some cases. However, foreign ownership of financial service firms was not liberalized by the 1989 reforms. Thus, the regulations under NAFTA represent a significant opportunity for foreign entities to participate in the Mexican financial sector.

Under NAFTA, a U.S. or Canadian investor (individual or corporation) may hold a 100% stake in a Mexican financial institution. The limits for U.S. and Canadian investors are stated in terms of total industry capital within specific industries, instead of the capital of an individual institution. The five different financial services industries are:
- Banks
- Securities firms
- Insurance companies
- Factors and leasing companies
- Limited-scope finance companies

The ownership restrictions are two-tiered. The first tier is the extent to which a single **foreign investor** (individual or corporation) may control industry capital. The second tier is the extent to which all **foreign investors** may control industry capital.

In the **banking sector** before NAFTA, investment by individual foreign investors had been limited to 5% of capital of the institution in question.

Aggregate investment by all foreign investors was limited to 30% of capital of the institution in question. During NAFTA's transition period from 1994 through 1999, no single investor may own more than 1.5% of banking industry capital. Beginning January 1, 2000, this ceiling is increased to 4% of Mexican banking capital. During the same transition period, the aggregate limit of the ownership of Mexican bank capital by foreign institutions begins at 8% in 1994 and increases each year to 15% in 1999. After 1999, there is no limit.

However, should the aggregate foreign share of Mexican banking capital reach 25%, Mexico has the option to freeze further foreign acquisitions for a period not to exceed three years. This option expires four years after the end of the transition period, that is, January 1, 2004. These provisions have the effect of containing (1) the extent to which an individual U.S. or Canadian firm may control the Mexican banking system and (2) the extent of foreign investment in the banking industry as a whole. This means that no individual foreign interest could represent a majority share of one of Mexico's larger banks. The aggregate restriction, at least through the year 2007, prevents foreign investors from assuming a dominating position through buying control of a large number of smaller Mexican banks.

In the **securities sector**, limits have been stipulated that are similar to those in the banking industry.[6] Prior to NAFTA, the individual limitation for securities firm ownership by foreign investors was 10% of the capital of the securities firm in question, while aggregate foreign ownership of a Mexican securities firm was limited to 30% of the Mexican firm's capital. Under NAFTA, during the transition period (1994 through 1999), individual U.S. and Canadian investors could control up to 4% of Mexican securities firm capital, representing a somewhat more liberal ceiling than in the case of commercial banks. During the transition period, the aggregate limit for foreign ownership of Mexican securities firms begins at 10% and increases to 20%. After the transition period, there is no limit.

As in the banking industry, there is also an option for a one-time freeze by the Mexican government in the securities industry. Between January 1, 2000 and January 1, 2004, the Mexican government may freeze further acquisition of Mexican securities firms by foreign investors for a period not to exceed three years. Nevertheless, the limits are generally more liberal in the securities industry than in the banking industry.

---

[6] It should be noted that the peso crisis, beginning in December, caused the acceleration of permissible foreign ownership of financial institutions.

In the **insurance sector**, before NAFTA, foreign investment was limited to 49% of a specific Mexican insurance company. There were no individual limits. Under NAFTA, the two-tiered limitations apply. During the transition period, a U.S. or Canadian investor may own no more than 1.5% of Mexican insurance company capital. During 1994, the first year of the transition period, foreign investors may own no more than 6% of aggregate Mexican insurance company capital. This percentage increased to 12% by 1999. After 1999, there were no such limitations.

Factors and leasing companies have fewer ownership restrictions. Before NAFTA, each individual company was limited to 49% foreign ownership. Under NAFTA, there are no individual limits with respect to U.S. or Canadian ownership of aggregate Mexican factoring and leasing companies, either during or after the transition period. The aggregate limit on foreign ownership during the transition period is 10% in the first year of the transition period, increasing to 20% by 1999. After 1999, there were no restrictions. In terms of ownership restrictions, factoring and leasing companies represent a greater opportunity to enter the Mexican financial system.

Limited-scope finance companies present an even greater opportunity than factoring and leasing companies with respect to entry into Mexico's financial system. Limited-scope finance companies are defined as those which offer services in consumer lending, commercial lending, mortgage lending, credit card services, or other lending services that are closely related to these. Before NAFTA, only the 49% limit on total foreign ownership of an individual company existed.

Under NAFTA, the ownership restriction are defined in a different manner vis-à-vis other financial institutions. The limitations are based on **assets** instead of **capital**. The aggregate limit is 3% throughout the transition period, with no limit thereafter. There is a distinctly different framework of ownership limitation in this sector — the 3% limit is a percentage of assets of both limited-scope finance companies and of commercial banks. Because of the extent to which the banking system dominates the Mexican financial services industry, this 3% limit on assets is a liberal ceiling for a fairly specialized form of financial institution.

The North American Free Trade Agreement represents a significant opportunity for investment in the financial structure of Mexico. The relatively liberal restrictions with respect to the limited-scope finance companies may reflect the desire of the Mexican government to cultivate those services offered by these companies. There is a realization that consumer, residential mortgage, and small- to medium-sized commercial customers have not been well served in the past. At the same time, the structure of the transition period allows Mexican banks and other financial institutions to become stronger before all foreign ownership restrictions are dropped.

The phase-in period also represents an opportunity for U.S. and Canadian banks to become established in one of these niches that were not being well served — in either the banking sector or in one of the other financial service sectors. The options are varied and interesting, particularly in light of the generally over banked condition of the United States. Under provisions of the North American Free Trade Agreement, Mexico represents an intriguing frontier for expansion and potential profitability.

References

Abbott, F. M. (2000). NAFTA and the legalization of world politics: A case study, *International Organization*, 54(3), 519–547.

Abu-Akeel, A. K. (1999). The MFN as it applies to service trade: New problems for an old concept. *Journal of World Trade*, 33(4), 103–129.

Ahn, D. (2000). Linkages between international financial and trade institutions — IMF, Workd Bank and WTO. *Journal of World Trade*, 34(4), 1–36.

Anonymous (1992). Three for free trade. *Canadian Banker*, 99(2), 6–10.

Anonymous. (2001). International developments and securities markets. *Norges Bank Financial Stability*, 1, 9–12.

Anonymous. (2001). The future of globalization of the financial services industry. *Journal of Taxation of Financial Institutions*, 14(3), 27 & 34.

Anonymous. (2001). The year ahead in global banking: Critical issues for 2001. *Global Finance*, 15(1), 32–33.

Atkinson, G. (1999). Developing global institutions: Lessons to be learned from regional integration experiences. *Journal of Economic Issues*, 33(2), 335–342.

Beddoes, Z. M. (1999). Global finance survey: A stitch in time. *The Economist*, 350(8104), S8–S12.

Bergsten, C. F. (2001). Fifty years of trade policy: The policy lessons. *The World Economy*, 24(1), 1–13.

Bhagwati, J. (1998). The Capital Myth: The Difference Between Trade in Widgets and Dollars. *Foreign Affairs*, 3, 7–12.

Bieber, S. M., & Sanchez-Navarro, J. (1999). Doors wide open. *Business Mexico*, 9(9), 20–21.

Blaine, M. J. (2000). Policy responses to capital inflows: Lessons from Mexico. *International Journal of Public Administration*, 23(5–8).

Blount, E. (1999). Rethinking the framework. *ABA Banking Journal*, 91(12), 68–72.

Braga, C., Safadi, R., & Yeats, A. (1994). Regional integration in the Americas: Déjà vu all over again? *The World Economy*, 17(4), 577–601.

Chen, I. (2001). Mexico's maquiladoras go way south of the border. *Global Finance*, 15(2), 71–72.

Conger, L. (1994). Transition to transparency. *Institutional Investor*, 28(1), 111+.

Corado, C., & de Melo, J. (1986). An ex–ante model for estimating the impact on trade flows of a country's joining a customs union. *Journal of Developmental Economics*, 24(1), 153–166.

Cornelius, P. K. (2000). Trade in financial services, capital flows, and the value-at-risk of countries. *The World Economy*, 23(5), 649–672.

Drickhamer, D. (2000). Financial/professional service. *Industry Week*, 249(2), 37–46.

Ethier, W. J. (1998). Regionalism in a multilateral world. *The Journal of Political Economy*, 106(6), 1214–1245.

Ethier, W. J. (2001). The new regionalism in the Americas: A theoretical framework. *North American Journal of Economics and Finance*, 12(2), 159–172.

Harner, S. M. (2000). Financial services and WTO: Opportunities knock. *The China Business Review*, 27(2), 10–15.

Hazera, A. (2000). Recent trends in the evolution of Mexican financial groups. *International Journal of Public Administration*, 23(5–8), 1007–1034.

Honegger, P., Isler, P., & Pulver, U. (2000). Banking and finance — Switzerland: A Legal Guide. *International Financial Law Review*, 7–11.

Ioannou, L. (1994). Better banking with NAFTA. *International Business*, 7(1), 40+.

Kelsey, C. (2000). The shape of financial services in Europe. *LIMRA's marketFacts*, 19(3), 12–14.

LaWare, J. P. (1993). Statements to Congress. *Federal Reserve Bulletin*, 79(11), 1031+.

Mattoo, A. (2000). Financial services and the WTO: Liberalisation commitments of the developing and transition economies. *The World Economy*, 23(3), 351–386.

Middlemiss, J. (2001). A uniform approach. *Bank Systems & Technology*, 38(5), 30–32.

Mondellini, L. (1999). Ford: Seeking benchmark status. *Euromoney*, 364, 48–49.

Mooney, S. F. (2001). Is financial services de-conglomeration in store? *National Underwriter*, 105(19), 54–56.

Morales, R., & Quandt, C. (1992). The new regionalism: Developing countries and regional collaborative competition. *International Journal of Urban and Regional Research*, 16(3), 462+.

Myers, J. G. (2000). Canada: Supplement: Banking Yearbook 2000. *International Financial Law Review*, 63–66.

Pasquero, J. (2000). Regional market integration in North America and corporate social management. *Business and Society*, 39(1), 6–23.

Price, D. M., & Christy, P.B. (1995). United States Legal Guide to Corporate Activity: Investing in North America. *International Financial Law Review*, Supp., 37.

Robson, P. (1993). The new regionalism and developing countries. *Journal of Common Market Studies*, 31(3), 329–349+.

Rogers, J. E. (1993). NAFTA dispute settlement for the finance sector. *Business Mexico*, 3(6), 40+.

Sauve, P. (2000). Developing countries and the GATS 2000 round. *Journal of World Trade*, 34(2), 85–92.

Sczudlo, R. S. (1993). NAFTA: Opportunities abound for US and Canadian financial institutions. *The Banker's Magazine*, 176(4), 28–32+.

Spero, K., & Caja, R. A. (1999). Getting caught by GATT. *Journal of Financial Planning*, 12(9), 72–77.

Steinherr, A., & Peree, E. (1999). How strong is the case for free trade in financial services? Walking the tightrope between domestic stability and international shocks. *The World Economy*, 22(9), 1221–1232.

Thurston, C. (2001). Integrating e-finance: Where's the value? *Global Finance*, 15(2), 62–65.

Trachtman, J. P. (1997). Accounting standards and trade disciplines: irreconcilable differences? *Journal of World Trade*, 31(6).

Wickham, J. (2000). Toward a green multilateral investment framework: NAFTA and the search for models. *Georgetown International Environmental Law Review*, 12(3), 617–646.

Zekos, G. I. (1999). An examination of GATT/WTO arbitration procedures. *Dispute Resolution Journal*, 54(4), 72–76.

Chapter 2

Financial Transactions Without Borders

Introduction

As globalization continues in many other areas, financial services firms have moved cautiously to integrate the Internet. Financial services providers realize that wealth of opportunity the Internet provides comes with an equal potential for risk. Financial services providers must consider both the benefits and the costs. While costs of a web-based access point are lower than the traditional brick-and-mortar branch, the associated investment in personnel, equipment, and technology can still be substantial. Additional risk management and strategic planning resources are required. The return on investment must justify the investment.

Since the inception of monetary systems, bankers worked to add value to the provision of financial services. The banking system has evolved into a highly structured, well-organized, often conservative conglomeration of organizations in the business of wealth management. Regulation can impact the payments system in unpredictable ways. Change does not come easily, but must prove efficient and stable before it is readily and universally accepted. Electronic banking applications have met with both resistance and enthusiasm. However as treaties such as the General Agreement on Trade in Services have provided greater market access, the atmosphere for cooperation in the development and advancement of services in electronic banking has been enhanced. Electronic banking — current applications and breakthroughs — will have significant impact on traditional services and future expansion of these services.

Electronic Banking

With the relaxation of trade restrictions, it is necessary to refine the systems of cross-border banking. For example, one of the provisions of the North American Free Trade Agreement speaks to is the free flow of information across borders and the ease of data processing that is necessary in the normal course of business.

Check Clearing

After cash, **checks** are the most preferred method of payment in the Unites States. Worldwide, it has been estimated that the daily settlement of checking account balances in the United States and abroad amounts to approximately two trillion dollars. In the United States alone, approximately two billion checks are written each day.

U.S. banks use the Federal Reserve System and its 12 regional offices to clear these checks. Fedwire is a high-speed electronic communications network (operated by the Federal Reserve Bank of New York) that links banks with the Federal Reserve Board of Governors, the 12 Federal Reserve District Banks and their 24 branches, the U.S. Treasury Department, and other federal agencies. Fedwire is the largest dedicated network in operation in the United States.

CHIPS (Clearinghouse Interbank Payments System), owned and operated by the New York Clearinghouse Association, transfers large amounts for interbank settlements. This computerized funds transfer system links 140 depository institutions and is used primarily for international dollar payments, accounting for 90% of the interbank payments relating to international trade.

In Canada, the check clearing function is much different. Since the system is highly concentrated, a small number of banks account for 90% of all bank assets and the vast majority of checks written. Accordingly, Canadian banks have large nationwide networks. Through these networks and reciprocal agreements, consumer checks are cleared on a same-day basis, despite the fact that actual settlement occurs the next day. Writers of checks in denominations of $50,000 or more (business transactions) are assessed any float costs that might accrue.

In Mexico, there are three clearinghouses, one each in Mexico City, Guadalajara, and Monterrey. The largest banks, which account for the majority of check clearing activity in Mexico use encoded checks that can be mechanically scanned during the clearing process. However, smaller banks have not adopted this practice.

In Europe, most countries have a **giro system** that performs the function of checking accounts in the United States. A giro system is a non-bank payments system (frequently at the post office) that transfers funds from one account to another on a same-day basis. Interestingly, the giro system of the United Kingdom is not used as frequently as its continental European counterparts. This is partially because the U.K. Post Office Giro system was not introduced until 1968. More fundamentally, however, British clearing banks have long emphasized personal banking services — branching nationwide and encouraging the use of checks. The four major U.K. banks dominate the retail banking market, controlling 80% of all personal bank accounts. They are HSBC Holdings, National Westminster, Barclays Bank, and Lloyds Bank (Price & Christy 1995)

In contrast, in Japan, checks and giro transactions originate almost exclusively in the business sector. Japanese payments are much more frequently in the form of cash or electronic transfer. The Japanese postal savings system has no parallel in the United States. This system accumulates savings from individuals and small businesses. The postal savings system is the largest savings bank in the world and, in the mid-1990s, represented approximately 17% of total assets of the banking system of Japan. It is a popular outlet for savings because the interest income was tax-exempt until 1988 and because there are many more locations, compared to bank branches.

Increasing Efficiencies in Check Clearing

Through **electronic check presentment (ECP),** information on a check may be shared electronically much faster than the physical check can be cleared. Electronic check presentment (ECP) is the process of clearing checks in which information from the magnetic ink character recognition (MICR) line — rather than the physical checks — is exchanged. The MICR line is machine-readable character string used to encode checks so that they can be read electronically by a reader/sorter. MICR information includes the identifying number of the bank on which the check is drawn, routing information, and the serial number of the check.

With ECP, the payee bank (bank in which the check has been deposited) scans the MICR line. This information is wired to the payor bank (bank upon which the check has been written). If there are insufficient funds for the check, the check is flagged overnight instead of several days, or even a week, later. The U.S. Federal Reserve System is also examining the ECP technology.

The Federal Reserve has long been a champion of further efficiencies in the payments system, actively encouraging truncation — the ultimate efficiency in check processing. When check truncation is employed, canceled checks are held by the payor's bank or by another bank in the check clearing process, rather than being returned in the account statement. A Federal Reserve Bank can either **truncate** checks at the bank of first deposit or. Excluding canceled checks from customer statements saves the payor bank at least $1 per account per month. Given the thousands of accounts maintained by most banks, the savings can be substantial.

Under the electronic check-clearing program of the Federal Reserve — available in all 12 Federal Reserve Bank districts — paper checks may follow the electronic exchange of payment data. However, if the bank requests, the Federal Reserve Bank will not forward the paper checks, but instead record microfilm copies or other images of the checks for later access by banks or their customers.

Employing **imaging technology** in check clearing means that a bank would receive graphical images of the checks drawn against it instead of the actual paper check. In this process, an electronic picture (image) of a check is created and transmitted during the check clearing process instead of shipping the physical check. The U.S. Federal Reserve also has much interest in this technology because it can provide backup support for truncating. Using images can assist the payor bank in such areas as pay-or-no-pay decisions and signature verifications.

The biggest technical challenge in imaging the check clearing process is the correct interpretation of the written check amounts. **Character amount recognition or character amount read (CAR)** means that personnel need not manually read the numerals written in the courtesy amount boxes of checks. The challenge is that there are as many as 30 different ways that checks are written. The problems with CAR tend to center around three factors:

- The condition or readability of the physical checks
- The various ways that customers write checks
- The variety of locations for the courtesy amount box on the checks

Imaging technology significantly improves the work environment in the check processing area. Typically, in this fast-paced operational area, two people who want to speak to each other must shout to be heard. With imaging technology, the same people may whisper and still hear each other. At the same time, the speed of processing has dramatically increased over conventional systems. An average, conventional check-clearing operation can clear about 1,400 checks per hour. An imaging system clears more than 20,000 per hour.

Electronic Payments and Inter-bank Networks

Electronic payments are effected through **automated clearinghouses (ACHs)** or through **wire transfers**. ACHs are computer-based clearing and settlement facilities for exchange of electronic debits and credits among financial institutions. ACH entries are often substituted for recurring payments (such as mortgage payments) or in the direct-deposit distribution of federal and corporate benefit payments (such as Social Security payments). Increasingly, this form of payment also is being used as a payment processor for payments within the corporate sector. Federal Reserve Banks provide the data processing services for most ACHs. Funds are available for withdrawal on a next-day basis.

Wire transfers are direct, electronic payments that usually involve large dollar payments between financial institutions. Fedwire and CHIPS provide these services. These funds are available for withdrawal on a same-day basis.

The Society for Worldwide Interbank Financial Telecommunications (SWIFT) is a nonprofit, cooperative organization that facilitates the exchange of payments messages, but not the payments, between more than 1,000 financial institutions in Europe and North America. SWIFT was developed as a more efficient alternative to telex or mail. Today, it is a widely used system for the secure transmittal of financial data. A SWIFT transaction is not a payment, but instead is an advice or instruction to transfer funds of a specified amount at another bank. The actual exchange of funds takes place on the domestic clearing system. The respective domestic clearinghouses then handle advices for payments by domestic banks to their correspondent banks in other countries.

The Internet is helping non-financial companies streamline the logistics of buying, selling and delivering products and services. However, payments are not necessarily as fast as the sales. Many companies today can receive orders, make deliveries, and issue invoices within a 24-hour period. However, they may still wait 45–60 days for payments in a system that remains the same as it was nearly fifty years ago. A study called "Optimizing the Financial Supply Chain," estimates that improved Internet-based billing and cash management could save the world's 30,000 largest companies approximately $90 billion a year (McCrary 2001).

Electronic bill payment and presentment software has made some headway into corporate accounting and purchasing departments. By letting customers pay bills over the Web, **electronic bill payment and presentment (EBPP)** can reduce a company's paper-based billing cycle from months to days and dramatically improve cash flow. By applying e-payment techniques internally, companies can streamline their purchasing and approval processes for expenses such as office supplies and corporate travel. Thus far, electronic bill presentment has been relatively disappointing despite its potential efficiencies for both businesses and consumers. Presentment capabilities let payers view their bills. Early efforts produced static bills with little or no ability to access or modify line items. That capability, sought by consumers, is a necessity for businesses, which follow strict accounting procedures. Early efforts toward e-payment did not inspire much confidence (Robinson 2001).

Banks and other financial institutions, however, are in a good position to help expand such services, according to a recent research study by Needham MA TowerGroup. recently indicates. "Integration of bill payment within EBPP is a natural fit for financial institutions such as credit unions and banks, which have strong relationships with both high-volume billers (such as utilities or telecommunications companies) and payers. ... While investment in EBPP will be significant, the potential reward for financial services institutions is great. In the business-to-consumer market alone, TowerGroup projects the ultimate conversion from paper to EBPP processes will generate a net revenue gain of $1.4 billion for financial institutions." (Merrick 2001)

Retail Applications

Technology also affects transactions by individual customers, primarily through **automated teller machines (ATMs)** and **point-of-sale (POS) systems.** The Cirrus Network, owned by MasterCard, allows funds to be withdrawn from an account at 80,000 ATMs in the United States. The Cirrus network is located in Denver and is connected to a number of other networks around the country:

- NYCE Automated Teller Machine Network in New York
- MAC Network in New York
- Yankee Network in New England
- STAR in California
- The National Plus Network, owned by Visa International

Electronic banking affects every facet of the banking system today in the United States. The networks in Canada are as well defined and developed as those in the United States. In fact, since the Canadian banking system is composed of relatively few banks vis-à-vis that of the United States, the Canadian ATM system complements its nationwide system of branches and is perhaps even more efficient than that in the United States. On the other hand, in Mexico 70% of the ATMs are controlled by just two banks — Banamex (30%) and Bancomer (40%). The Mexican retailing banking market has not been developed to its full potential (clarke 1996).

In retail banking, POS electronic links accomplish the same outcome as wire transfers. However, while wire transfers typically involve large denominations, POS transactions are geared to the smaller denomination, high-volume retail market. Examples of such applications include grocery stores and service stations. A POS transaction is effected through the use of a debit card, which results in reduction of the payor's bank account balance (that is, a "debit" to deposit account of the payor) and a "credit" to the deposit account of the payee. After initial start-up costs for the banks involved, POS significantly reduces the cost of check processing by the participating institutions. This is still a growing area of technological applications in retail banking.

Electronic commerce is the term applied to activities involving the exchange of goods or services for value over a computer network or automated system. As significant participants in the payments system, financial institutions are becoming more aggressive in adopting electronic banking capabilities that include sophisticated marketing systems, remote-banking capabilities, and stored value programs. This area is highly dynamic as emerging technologies yield a variety of delivery alternatives and innovative products and services.

Smart cards are portable computing devices with small programmable data store and certain tamper-resistance capabilities. They are embedded in a plastic card that looks like a traditional magnetic stripe credit card. They can be utilized in several way — identification, medical records, consumer profiling, and financial services and banking applications. Smart cards have been popular in Europe for several years, but have been relatively slow to catch on in the United State. Privacy is one of the reasons typically cited. Many people fear having so much information stored in one place. Yet several different organizations have started introducing the smart card as part of their everyday business. Target, the discount retailer, recently launched its own smart card product tied to its store credit Visa card (M'Raihi & Yung 2001).

From the perspective of financial institutions, smart cards with magnetic strips represent less of a shift in technology than smart cards with computer chips. Retailers with whom the banks cooperate in POS facilities have invested heavily in magnetic strip technology. Such retailers include oil companies (service stations), national food chains, and national department store chains. A move to chip cards will represent significant costs for a large-scale transition.

Another issue for financial institutions and the development of smart card technology is **Regulation E (Reg E)**, the Federal Reserve regulation that sets rules, liabilities, and procedures for electronic funds transfers (EFT). Reg E also establishes consumer protections in EFTs. One of these protections is that receipts are generally required to document EFTs. This provision must be addressed before smart cards can be used to, for example, transfer funds between bank and securities accounts or settle insurance claims.

Bank Management Applications

The earliest application of computers within the internal banking system was the use of large mainframe computers to maintain the general ledger, loan, and deposit systems. When personal computers were introduced into the banking environment, the first uses were for office automation, spreadsheets, and word processing.

The most current application of computer technology within the bank is **client-server architecture**. This configuration allows the sharing of information and software among the many users of the system. Part of this software is now electronic mail, or e-mail. In a bank that is technologically up-to-date, as much as 70% of internal written communication is done through e-mail. The modern commercial bank must be able to change and add elements to its computer software and hardware systems.

As the profit emphasis in banking has shifted away from the interest rate spread and toward the generation of fee income, there has been increased emphasis on derivatives and derivative trading. Thus, software that enables **the *pricing and valuation of derivatives*** and their component parts also has become an integral part of the commercial bank computer architecture (Thurston 2001).

Systems of commercial banks must be able not only to keep track of loans and deposits but also to **track performance**. Analyses of individual client relations are best conducted with the help of systems that summarize all activity of each individual client. Each department then has a better sense of the services that are, or are not, being offered to a client throughout the bank. Alternatively, the officer that is responsible for that client relationship is more knowledgeable and can provide better service. Even mundane tasks, such as accounts payable, can be incorporated into the computer system by permitting the scanning of invoices when received. In this way, the payment process is updated on a continuous basis and made far more efficient (Robinson 2001).

Expanding Scope of Applications

The importance of electronic networks in banking goes beyond the retail market and funds transfer between institutions and corporations. The actual facilitation of trade has begun to center on technology. Until recently, very little had changed in the way of trade finance for over 1,000 years. However, now the most recent innovations in trade finance involve **electronic data interchange (EDI)**. This technology is still in the early stages, but promises to be the method through which international trade and finance are conducted in the future. Typically, banks have used electronic systems in their trade finance in one of three ways:

- Generation and communication of documentation (document imaging and work flow are the newest developments)
- Payment transfers (through SWIFT or telex)
- Finalization of the bookkeeping process

However, these processes were confined to interbank transactions. The latest innovation in this field is the establishment of corresponding systems of technology in the customer's facility.

At this point, systems established on client premises are being introduced for only the largest customers. However, as is true with many technological innovations, what is now rare and unusual will become, at some point in the future, commonplace and typical. Currently, these systems enable customers to complete a number of trade transactions from their own locations:

- *Make application for trade finance*
- *Transfer documentation electronically*
- *Generate letters of credit electronically*

Examples of those banks that are now offering such EDI systems are Barclays in the United Kingdom (TradeManager), Hong Kong and Shanghai Banking Corporation in the United Kingdom and in Hong Kong (Hexagon), and Citibank in the United States (Citibanking). Citibanking is Citibank's system. Through a single window, Citibanking permits Citibank customers to access information about trade, cash management and securities. Citibanking customers may make inquiries about their import and export letters of credit and collections. Through EDI, they may initiate transactions, monitor the status of these transactions, receive up-to-date verification of their financial obligations, and generate various reports.

Requiring a customer to establish an electronic system that will tie into a bank's system represents a large commitment for the bank client and has several effects. It tends to:

- *Commit the customer to one bank*
- *Form a basis for future electronic interfaces*
- *Greatly increase the efficiency with which trade finance can be conducted*

As such systems are developed and placed in operation, some form of standardization will inevitably result. This standardization will make it easier for clients to interface with more than one bank and for a variety of purposes (McCrary 2001).

Retail Banking

The need both to reduce costs and to deliver more efficient service to customers constitutes a real challenge in retail banking. Bank employees are the contact point between the institution and the public. Severe staff reductions and promised future reductions create low morale among the bank staff. Under such conditions, there is real concern that productivity and customer service will suffer.

There are a number of questions that should be answered in the process of reengineering the retail banking function. None of them focus precisely on cost. Instead, cost is one of the methods of evaluating an alternative. Cost is only one half of the cost/benefit relationship. No bank, indeed, no company of any kind in any part of the world, can survive only by reducing costs. Unless there is growth in the market, a bank will not be sustained in the long run. A successful reengineering will, at a minimum, address the following issues:

- *Attracting customers*
- *Assessing customer needs*
- *Delivery of services*
- *Retaining existing customers*
- *Active feedback from customers*
- *Employee loyalty*

The revolution in retail banking is driven fundamentally by increased competition domestically and internationally. Costs must be reduced if banking institutions are to remain competitive with other providers of financial services. However, without the advent and availability of technological support, the revolution in retail banking would be much less far-reaching. Virtually every element of the banking industry is touched by technology and the power associated with it. Most notably, this includes the use of electronic cards, phone banking, the Internet, and multimedia kiosks.

The information that can be provided by enhanced interaction between accounts could be considered a goldmine. The profit-generating model of many of the dot-coms in the 1990's, was based on the premise that the aggregation of information on clientele was indeed valuable. It was hoped that this information, once gathered, could provide better target marketing data, individualization of the retail and information experience, and eventual creation of a global online market place. Failure came in both the implementation of the process and the analysis of the data. The Primary issues were that people did not necessarily "click through" on advertising, the Internet didn't necessarily provide enough business for many companies that depended solely on Internet business, many underestimated privacy as a significant issue to the consumer, and several other seemingly minor issues. However, over time, these small issues created a cascading effect that brought the technology bull market to its knees.

A California-based online marketing service, Encirq, has launched Illuminated Statements, a **proprietary desktop technology** that allows enhanced interaction between consumers' online credit card and checking accounts, banks and merchants. Encirq also hopes that this new software package will be a better paradigm for aggregating data from consumers. The idea is to make online statements interactive portals that offer both simplified expense reports and enhanced communication capabilities with merchants and banks. With this information base, Encirq believes financial institutions can benefit by converting what was once thought of as a cost center into powerful marketing opportunities. Of course, the privacy provisions of the 199 **Financial Services Modernization Act (Gramm-Leach Bliley)** require complete disclosure of the way such information is shared with other subsidiaries of the firm and with other firms (Gruenwedel 2000).

While many may not see the immediate value of such information gathering, it does allow financial institutions to eventually enhance customer relations and retention – for existing and future customers. This becomes exceedingly important as many retail financial institutions move into other areas of financial services. Relationship marketing continues to prove effective.

Trade Finance

Online business-to-business e-commerce volumes are expected to increase dramatically. There exists an immediate need for online payment capabilities. Yet there still exists no single solution that addresses the end-to-end payment process, from invoice issuance and tracking to reconciliation between banks, corporations, and exchanges. While pieces of the whole process have been mapped out and brought to fruition, integration has not been accomplished. Several factors contribute to slow development. Switching costs have been high from the standpoint of many businesses. Some are waiting to see which end of the value chain will push the move to electronic trade finance. Several smaller, less technologically advanced markets may not have the financial resources and expertise to compete actively once these integrations begin to take place.

This is not to say that innovations are not occurring or that the level of services is not expanding. In January 2001, Visa International launched Visa Commerce, a new solution suite designed to implement seamless and secure online e-payment functionalities in business-to-business (B2B) transactions. This launch was an integral part of Visa International's long-term program designed to provide solutions to businesses' needs for secure e-payments. Visa has also introduced a B2B Internet payment solution, the Open Account, that facilitates e-payments between financial institutions and non-financial corporations. More new products are expected to be introduced in the future that will complement this business solution (Chapel 2001).

On the international front, payment methodologies are changing as well. International electronic trade is a reality and major exporters and importers are conducting trade on-line. There are thousands of business-to-business e-marketplace sites operating today, trading everything from bananas to zinc. Of course, many of these will not exist long-term, largely because of a lack of liquidity. The survivors will be those sites that have strong logistical support and involvement from key players in the industry — producers, traders or financiers. Resolving existing logistical challenges will drive the future of e-trade, and important matters relating to standardization of documentation and communication, security and legal requirements on a vast range of issues, such as title to goods, require the utmost attention. There is also the need to incorporate insurance, corporate ratings, inspection services and customs procedures, not to mention the most appropriate financing mechanisms. Two of the best-known trading platforms, Bolero.net and TradeCard, have worked hard to refine their systems. Bolero.net was created in 1999 as part of a global initiative to move trade onto the Internet. The network incorporates financial institutions represented by the Society for Worldwide Interbank Financial Telecommunication (SWIFT) and the world's logistics community represented by the Through Transport (TT)

Club. The Bolero system provides secure electronic transmission of business data and documents along the entire trade chain from front-end order processing and management to back-end trade document exchange. Bolero.net is the trading name of Bolero International (Soydemir 2000).

But these trading platforms seek to provide an efficient and secure communication standard that will facilitate cross-border transactions by converting required paper documents involved in the transaction chain to electronic equivalents within a secure environment. Many international banks involved in trade are either partners with such trading platforms, or are keeping a close eye on developments, while at the same time preparing to embrace the transition to electronic transactions. This is not an easy process - moving from a backroom paper shuffling system to straight through electronic processing requires the right products, reorganization and time.

Letters of Credit

A **letter of credit (L/C)** is a document, usually issued by a bank upon instructions from the buyer of goods that permits the seller of goods to draw a specified sum of money under specified terms. These specified terms typically specify receipt by the bank of certain documents that evidence compliance with terms of the transaction within a given period of time. When the bank accepts drafts that are drawn under a letter of credit, such acceptance assures the seller (or the seller's bank) that the claim will be satisfied.

There are several characteristics of letters of credit:
- *Irrevocable*
- *Confirmed vs. Unconfirmed*
- *Revolving*
- *Transferable*
- *Acceptance Credit*

A letter of credit is most often irrevocable. This means that the exporter is assured that the credit will be available. Banks should generally advise their clients not to accept letters of credit that are revocable. Such an arrangement can be canceled or altered by the drawee after it has been issued by the drawee's bank. On the other hand, before the date of expiration, an irrevocable credit cannot be canceled, revoked, or withdrawn without the consent of the party in whose favor the credit is granted.

Quite often a U.S. company will require that a letter of credit be confirmed. This is most often the case when an exporting company is accepting a letter of credit from a country that has a higher risk profile, that is, represents higher risk of nonpayment. Confirmation is a method of enhancing the foreign bank's credit status. The beneficiary of a letter of credit (exporter) may request a local bank to confirm the letter of credit of the foreign bank. Confirmation means that the local (confirming) bank assumes responsibility for payment of all drafts under the letter of credit. This is an added assurance for the exporting firm. In the absence of this process, the letter of credit is unconfirmed.

A revolving letter of credit describes the method in which the credit may be available. A revolving letter of credit may be revocable, irrevocable, confirmed, or unconfirmed. A revolving credit will stipulate:

* *Maximum total value available under the line of credit*
* *Maximum individual payments under the letter of credit*
* *Dates for which these values are relevant*
* *Final termination date of the letter*

In a revolving credit, it is incumbent upon the importer or the user of the letter of credit to properly time all charges against the letter of credit to avoid exceeding any specified maximum stipulated in the letter of credit.

A transferable letter of credit is one under which a beneficiary has the right to give instructions to the accepting bank (or to any bank that is entitled to effect negotiations) to make the credit available to one or more third parties. This is a "trader" or middleman credit. Alternatively, a seller/exporter may use a transferable credit to pay a subcontractor. The beneficiary of a transferable credit has the right, within the constraints outlined in the letter of credit, to transfer the credit to suppliers anywhere. The credit essentially becomes a way for a trader to pay for goods that it sells to an ultimate buyer and obtains from an original supplier. The credit typically is set at the value equal to that which the ultimate buyer agrees to pay. The amount of the credit that is transferred is the amount that the supplier of the goods has agreed to accept as payment for the goods. When the supplier of goods presents documents that indicate that the goods have been satisfactorily delivered to the ultimate buyer, the suppliers invoice is paid and the trader or middleman receives the difference.

An acceptance credit is sometimes referred to as a "term credit" or "usance credit." The acceptance credit is perhaps the mostly widely used in that it substitutes the credit of the importer's bank for the credit of the importer itself. In this situation, the exporter (drawer) draws a draft on the accepting bank, which draft is accepted, typically, by the importer's bank (drawee). The drawee will accept the draft when all terms and conditions specified in the letter of credit have been satisfied. The process of acceptance guarantees payment to the exporter on the due date. At any time after acceptance, it is also possible for the exporter to receive payment prior to the due date by discounting the draft at the face amount less interest.

There are a number of ways in which U.S. banks can participate in the L/C market without establishing locations in Mexico or Canada. When a U.S. exporter receives a letter of credit it is typically through an "advising" bank. The process of advising is often no more involved than a U.S. bank placing a note with the letter of credit from a foreign bank, indicating that the letter of credit is authentic. For this service, an advising bank will receive $50 to $150.

Negotiating a letter of credit is the process of examining documents after shipment and paying according to the letter of credit. Typically, the advising bank is also the negotiating bank. In terms of timeliness and ease of communication, the interests of a U.S. exporter are best served when a U.S. bank, or at least a U.S. office of a foreign bank, negotiates a letter of credit. The typical fee for negotiating ranges from .125% to .5% of the amount of the letter of credit.

As noted earlier, confirmation is the process through which a local bank assumes responsibility for payment in the event that a less-well-known, more risky foreign bank does not pay according to the terms of the L/C. The typical fee for confirming is between .125% and 3.0%. However, if the foreign bank is extremely risky, a U.S. bank should be cautious about confirming its letters of credit. Also, a confirming bank will should have an open line of credit between itself and the foreign bank in question.

Bills of Exchange

A **bill of exchange** is an unconditional written order that requires one party to whom it is addressed to pay on demand, or at some future date, a sum of money to the order of a named party or bearer. The bill of exchange is the general classification in which acceptances and commercial bank drafts are classified. A bill of exchange is considered dishonored if it is not accepted by the drawee or not paid by drawee. At such time that a bill of exchange is refused, "noting" is the process of having the bill dated and initialed by a notary public. Collection of the bill then proceeds through appropriate legal channels.

The two types of bills are sight bill and usance bill of exchange. A sight bill is payable on demand, that is, at sight or on presentation. A usance bill is payable on a specified date in the future or on a determinable date in the future, for example, 180 days after sight. In order to qualify as a bill of exchange, an instrument must be specific with respect to date of payment and amount of payment. Note that bills of exchange can be used in the context of a letter of credit. When a draft (bill of exchange) is drawn under a letter of credit, then subsequently accepted, it becomes a banker's acceptance (BA).

Forfaiting

Forfaiting is a form of supplier credit in which an exporter surrenders possession of export receivables, which are usually guaranteed by a bank in the importer's country, by selling them at a discount to a forfaiter in exchange for cash. These instruments may also carry the guarantee of the foreign government. In a forfaiting transaction, an exporter approaches a forfaiter before completing a transaction. Once the forfaiter commits to the deal and sets the discount rate, the exporter can incorporate the discount into the selling price. Forfaiters usually work with bills of exchange or promissory notes, which are unconditional and easily transferable debt instruments that can be sold on the secondary market.

- *Forfaiting is the purchase, without recourse, of receivables from the export sales of goods. This is similar to factoring (the sale of receivables for immediate cash) with two important differences:*
- *Factoring involves credit terms that typically do not exceed 180 days; forfaiting can cover several years.*
- *Factoring does not protect against political risk or transfer risk; forfaiting does.*
- *Forfaiting is a competitive financing alternative in many developing countries where hard currency is scarce and is important in Mexico, South America, Asia, and parts of Eastern Europe.*

The origins of forfaiting can be traced back to periods prior to World War II (WWII). However, this form of financing did not reach high levels of acceptance or become widely used until after the war. Aval is the payment of a bill of exchange or promissory note that has been endorsed by the signature of a third party (usually a bank) that appears on the bill, which endorsement guarantees payment in the event of default by purchaser of goods. After WWII, many war-torn Eastern European countries needed to import grain, primarily from the United States. At the same time, there was a real scarcity of foreign exchange. Swiss bankers stepped in to finance these transactions. In the process, they bought the bills of exchange of U.S. and other suppliers without recourse, after they satisfied themselves that there was adequate assurance of aval. The Swiss bankers than presented the bills up for payment at the maturity date. Thus, the origin of forfaiting is as a Swiss-based method of financing grain deliveries.

Over time, the former Soviet Union and other Eastern European countries faced consistently difficult situations with respect to hard currency availability. The list of items that were financed through forfaiting expanded into a full range of commodities, products, capital goods, and large projects. Today, forfaiting activity is most heavily concentrated in London, which may be seen as the forfaiting capital of the world. Now major banks, with several U.S. banks offering the service worldwide, offer the service also (Wright 2001).

The instruments that are used in forfaiting are either bills of exchange or promissory notes. The bill of exchange or promissory note is inscribed with per aval, signed, and completed in the name of the party on whose behalf the aval is being provided. Technically, the avalist assumes the role of party that commits to make the payment. From the perspective of the forfaiter, the avalist becomes the debtor. The aval then is a simply form of guarantee for the forfaiter. This procedure is according to the old Code Napoleon. In international circles, there is no standardized guarantee. However, there are certain elements that must be contained in the aval. For example, the guarantee must be assignable and transferable to permit the forfaiter to trade the debt in the secondary market, if so desired. It must indicate that the aval is unconditional. Thus, the aval and the letter of guarantee are the traditional forms of security for forfaiters.

There is also a secondary market in forfaiting circles. The paper that is generated can be sold in the secondary market to help spread the risk of the forfaiter and to increase the forfaiter's liquidity.

As trade finance continues to modernize, accountability and rate of return on investment are becoming more important to many companies. Coincidentally, the forfait market is very quiet at the moment. It seems that companies are shying away from forfaiting in favor of other financial products that are more transparent when dealing with larger sums. For some traditional trade financiers it may be necessary to separate trade finance from trade payments in order to pull in more business (Wright 2001). Various nontraditional financing techniques may be used to solve a customer's trade problems besides forfaiting. Nontraditional, or structured, trade finance covers an array of financial, commercial, and documentary techniques to diversify against risks in the financing of global trade. Because the structure often involves numerous counter parties in one sale or a series of sale transactions, nontraditional trade finance effort is highly proactive, compared to the more reactive, traditional trade finance approach of dealing with one counterpart.

Countertrade

International **countertrade** is a practice in which a supplier commits contractually, as a condition of sale, to reciprocate and undertake certain specified commercial initiatives that compensate and benefit the buyer. Almost all countertrade activities are influenced by government intervention or scrutiny, either through legislation or through regulation at the ministerial level. Countertrade, or compensatory trade, is linked primarily to the inability of many developing countries to generate sufficient amounts of hard currency to purchase needed or desired imports. In some cases, countertrade is an alternative to no trade at all.

Countertrade is not appropriate for all exporters or for all types of trade transactions. Countertrade arrangements typically involve structuring deals that are tailor-made for the two sides of the transaction. This requires a large commitment of time and administrative resources. As a result, countertrade is most successful when undertaken either between countries that have an established relationship, by firms that have established foreign market positions, or by entities that have a substantial dollar value of transactions, together with substantial profit margins to absorb the administrative costs associated with countertrade.

Barter is the oldest firm of countertrade and is an exchange of goods for goods. It is a one-time arrangement under a single contract. There are no financial transfers involved in barter transactions. Typically, these arrangements are made on a government-to-government basis. If the needs of one party in the transaction do not match the goods that are supplied by the other party, it may be necessary to employ a third party broker to dispose of the goods on the world commodity markets. Brokers can also swap deliveries of equivalent commodities such as, for example, petroleum, for other clients around the world to save on transportation costs.

In buyback or compensation countertrade, the original exporter accepts as full or partial payment products that are derived from the original exported product. This process can support the construction and financing of productive facilities such as, for example, the export of machine and capital products. An early example of the buyback arrangement was seen in the early 20th century in the United Kingdom, France, and especially Germany. In these cases, chemical companies purchased feed stocks from other European countries with less well developed industrial infrastructures and returned to them a specified amount of finished products such as pharmaceuticals and fertilizers. Buyback arrangements have now been used to finance turnkey plants or retrofitting and modernization of manufacturing facilities in developing countries.

Counterpurchase is an agreement through which the original exporter will accept, as full or partial payment, products that are not related to the original exported product. The items most often involved in counterpurchase arrangements have been traditional exports, such as agricultural commodities, fertilizer, bulk chemicals, and minerals. In some cases, the transactions have also included industrial and chemical goods, coffee, and textiles.

An interesting aspect of countertrade has been in oil trading. In the 1970s, OPEC had begun to agree on quotas in terms of each member country's individual oil shipments.[7] As the price of oil increased, many of these producers wanted to sell more than their quota. Exchanging oil in countertrade transactions blurred the economic effect because the oil was not sold for cash. In the early 1980s, a Boeing 747 aircraft was exchanged for oil from Saudi Arabia. More recently, British Aerospace exchanged Saudi oil for Tornados. Since the mid-1980s, however, oil quotas have become less of a binding constraint and countertrade based on oil has declined in volume.

---

[7] OPEC is an acronym for Organization of Petroleum Exporting Countries.

Nevertheless, countertrading continues to be applied in various ways in many countries. A firm conducting countertrade has two choices with respect to organizational approach. It can either structure an in-house capability to negotiate and manage the transactions or it can solicit the help of an outside source. If a firm elects to adopt the in-house approach, a senior countertrader must be employed, along with two or three support staff, office support for that staff, and associated expenses. The associated expenses will include primarily telephone expense and substantial outlays for travel. A company should be prepared to devote $300,000 to $400,000 per year to maintain such an in-house facility.

If the company decides to use an outside countertrade service, the providers may be banks, trading houses, and/or consultants. Major banks in New York, London and Frankfurt have large and experienced countertrade departments, generally included with their trade finance activities. Most commercial banks participate in the process by providing financial support for the countertrade and do not accept a commodity risk (either ownership or responsibility for sale of the commodity). On the other hand, trading houses will accept the actual commodities. However, it is relatively difficult to find a trading house that will accept finished manufactured goods. Consultants can be helpful in finding parties for the countertrade transactions. Typically, consultants will not accept the responsibility for the commodities or the financing.

One of the attractive features of countertrade for banks is that it is actually a two-sided transaction. The two transactions are tied to each other and the bank can provide interim financing since the two transfers of goods typically will not take place at the same time. Handling the interim financing associated with the countertrade can be a good source of interest and fee income for commercial banks.

Securities Markets

Financial risk may be reduced through proper diversification of asset portfolios to help improve the risk/return trade-off. These assets can include cash, short-term debt instruments, bonds, and stock. Diversification of assets limits risk by spreading investments over a number of companies, industries, and/or countries. Portfolio variability is the extent to which the actual returns may be different from expected returns. When the rates of return of assets in a portfolio do not move in the same way, negative returns of some assets can be offset by positive returns of other assets.

Over the past decade, closed-end country funds have become a popular avenue to investors for diversifying into foreign stock markets. In contrast to global or regional closed-end funds, a country fund is an investment company that invests all of the shareholders' money in the common stocks of one foreign country. The fund issues a fixed number of shares in the United States in its initial public offerings. Investors can only buy shares of a fund in the public offerings and subsequently buy and sell the fund's outstanding shares through the New York Stock Exchange. The trading of these shares is the same as trading common stocks of other industrial companies. Hence, country fund investors obtain exposure to the country of their choice, while holding a diversified portfolio of foreign country stocks. Unlike a mutual fund, closed-end fund shareholders cannot redeem their shares to the closed end fund. The underlying value of a country fund's assets, called the net asset value, is the market value of all the stocks held in that foreign country expressed in U.S. dollars. Assuming security markets are efficient, frictionless, and internationally integrated, the market price and the net asset value of the country fund shares would be expected to be the same. Only four country funds existed at the beginning of 1986; the number of funds increased to about fifty by the end of 1998. The increase in the number of country funds could be due to the benefits of international diversification that country funds can offer. Several studies find there are diversification benefits from investing in country funds.

An important question concerning integration of global financial markets, as such investments become more popular is whether local investors in an equity market react differently from international investors, particularly during periods of financial crisis. Because local investors are closer to information, they might turn pessimistic before foreign investors before a crisis. A study of the Asian crisis of 1997 from Columbia University examined whether local investors in each of the 6 Asian stock markets - Indonesia, Korea, Malaysia, the Philippines, Taiwan and Thailand - reacted differently from international investors during the 1997 Asian financial crisis. Results indicate that international investors turned pessimistic before local investors (Sorin & Burton 2001).

References

Ahn, D. (2000). Linkages between international financial and trade institutions — IMF, World Bank and WTO. *Journal of World Trade*, 34(4), 1–36.

Anonymous. (2001). International developments and securities markets. *Norges Bank Financial Stability*, 1, 9–12.

Anonymous.(2001). The future of globalization of the financial services industry. *Journal of Taxation of Financial Institutions*, 14(3), 27 & 34.

Anonymous.(2001). The year ahead in global banking: Critical issues for 2001. *Global Finance*, 15(1), 32–33.

Anonymous. (2000). Financial world may still be in paddock as Internet technology races into far turn. *International Insurance Monitor*, 53(1), 17–18.

Bell, J. (2001). Spurring electronic trading. *Latinfinance (Coral Gables), Latin Banking Guide & Directory*, 2001, 32–33.

Bosch, R., Abegglen, S., & Baumgarten, M. O. (2000). E-banking: Supplement: Switzerland: A Legal Guide. *International Financial Law Review*, 19–23.

Brandman, J. (2000). Trade finance trails the Internet. *Global Finance*, 14(8), 34–35.

Cattani, C. F. (2000). Electronic finance: A cornerstone to trade and compete internationally. *International Trade Forum*, 3, 13–14.

Chapel, C. (2001). Visa bridges B2B e-payments. *Asian Business*, 37(1), 57.

Clarke, D. (1996). The dream of borderless banking. *Canadian Banker*, 103(1), 32–36.

Feinberg, P. (2001). Waiting to switch to new EAFE index could harm worldwide equity markets. *Pensions & Investments*, 29(22), 30+.

Gruenwedel, E. (2000). New marketing technology targets online banking statements. *Brandweek*, 41(21), 76+.

Gulen, H., & Mayhew, S. (2000). Stock index futures trading and volatility in international equity markets. *The Journal of Futures Markets*, 20(7), 661–685.

M'Raihi, D. & Yung, M. (2001). E-commerce application of smart cards. *Computer Networks*, 36(4), 453–472.

Macaluso, M. J., & Pillar, T. G. (2001). E-finance and cross-border transactions. *The Banking Law Journal*, 118(1), 41–47.

Mattoo, A. (2000). Financial services and the WTO: Liberalisation commitments of the developing and transition economies. *The World Economy*, 23(3), 351–386.

McCrary, E. S. (2001). Saving big bucks along the financial supply chain. *Global Finance*, 15(5), D.

Merrick, B. (2001). Financial institutions will drive EBPP. *Credit Union Magazine*, 67(8), 18.

Middlemiss, J. (2001). A uniform approach. *Bank Systems & Technology*, 38(5), 30–32.

Mondellini, L. (1999). Ford: Seeking benchmark status. *Euromoney*, 364, 48–49.

Mooney, S. F. (2001). Is financial services de-conglomeration in store? *National Underwriter*, 105(19), 54–56.

Nelson, K. (2000). New service helps retailers with returned checks. *Bank Systems & Technology*, 37(11), 27.

Price, D. M., & Christy, P.B. (1995). United States legal guide to corporate activity: Investing in North America. *International Financial Law Review*, Supp., 37.

Robinson, T. (2001). End the B2B paper chase – electronic bill payment is finally gaining momentum, as companies look to slash paper costs and improve cash flow. *Internetweek*, (881), 33–34.

Simpson, P. (2001). The international E-commerce evolution. *World Trade*, 14(6), 66–68.

Sorin, A. T., & Burton, Z. (2001). The effects of the Asian crisis on global equity markets. *The Financial Review*, 36(1), 125–140.

Soydemir, G. (2000). International transmission mechanism of stock market movements: Evidence from emerging equity markets, 19(3), 149–176.

Thurston, C. (2001). Integrating e-finance: Where's the value? *Global Finance*, 15(2), 62–65.

Trachtman, J. P. (1997). Accounting standards and trade disciplines: Irreconcilable differences? *Journal of World Trade*, 31(6).

Wright, R. (2001). All quiet on the forfait front. *The Banker*, 151(905), The World Top 1000 Banks 108–110.

Chapter 3

General Agreement on Trade in Services: Agreement on Financial Services

Introduction

The World Trade Organization oversees the implementation of the General Agreement of Trade in Services. "In brief, the World Trade Organization (WTO) is the only international organization dealing with the global rules of trade between nations. Its main function is to ensure that trade flows as smoothly, predictably and freely as possible" (http://www.wto.org).

Established in 1995, and operational by 1997, as the successor to the General Agreement on Tariffs and Trade (GATT), the World Trade Organization (WTO), is a relatively new organization established to administer and direct the multilateral trade system already begun by GATT. The central force of this system of trade consists of the agreements of the WTO, negotiated and signed by a large majority of the world's trading nations, and ratified (as necessary) in their parliaments or legislatures. These agreements are the legal ground-rules or contracts for international commerce that guarantee member countries important trade rights. They also bind governments to keep their trade policies within agreed limits to every country's benefit. The agreements were negotiated and signed by governments who have the choice not to join the WTO.

The current trading system administered and directed by the WTO was developed through a series of trade negotiations held under GATT. The first rounds dealt mainly with tariff reductions but later negotiations included other areas such as anti-dumping, workers' rights, and non-tariff measures. The 1986–94 Uruguay Round led to the creation of the WTO as the member countries formally agreed to create an umbrella organization to administer GATT. While the WTO to some extent replaces or formalizes the treaties formed under GATT, GATT continues as a new set of treaty terms under **GATT 2000**.

The goal of the World Trade Organization is simply to facilitate trade through administering trade agreements while acting as a forum for trade negotiations and settling trade disputes, reviewing national trade policies for consistency with current GATT agreements, and assisting developing countries in trade policy issues.

Background and Membership of the WTO

To date, the WTO has more than 140 members, accounting for over 90% of world trade. Over 30 other countries are negotiating membership. By lowering trade barriers, the World Trade Organization hopes to break down not only barriers to commerce but other barriers as well. It is hoped by the WTO that this multilateral trading system will provide a measure of assurance in the exchange of goods and services across the world. It is hoped that this assurance will also help bring member countries into better communication for the common good of the markets around the world.

Most member countries automatically became founder members of the WTO when it was established on January 1, 1995 because they had signed the Uruguay Round agreement in Marrakesh in April 1994. Others joined GATT after April 1994 but before the WTO was set up. Another group of countries participated in the Uruguay Round but did not complete their membership negotiations until 1995. All of these countries are considered original members as well. See Appendix 3–1 for a list of member countries as of January 2002.

Any fully autonomous country or territory may join the World Trade Organization through an application process called accession. This four-stage process begins when the government applying for membership drafts a **memorandum** that describes all aspects of its trade and economic policies that have a bearing on WTO agreements for submission to the WTO working party in charge of the country's application.

Once sufficient progress towards compliance to WTO policies and procedures is in place, **bilateral talks** between the applicant country and other members take place. Typically, these talks cover tariffs and specific market access, and policies in goods and services. The new member's commitments are to apply equally to all WTO members under normal non-discrimination rules.

Once the talks are completed, the Membership Terms are then drafted and the terms of accession are finalized. The treaty, called the **protocol of accession** and schedules of the potential new member's commitments are published in a report.

This **report is presented to the WTO General Council** for at least a two-thirds majority vote of the WTO membership. Then the new member country may sign the treaty. In some cases, the country's parliament must ratify the treaty before membership is complete.

Current Operations of the WTO

Typically, decisions are made by the entire membership by consensus. A majority vote is possible though it has never been used in the WTO, and was extremely rare under GATT. To date, the agreements of the WTO have been ratified in all members' parliaments. The WTO's top-level decision-making body is the **Ministerial Conference** that meets at least once every two years. Below this is the **General Council** (consisting typically of ambassadors and heads of delegations stationed in Geneva,Switzerland but sometimes of officials sent from members' capitals) that meets several times a year in the Geneva headquarters. The General Council also meets separately as the **Trade Policy Review Body** and the **Dispute Settlement Body** as needed. Reporting to the General Council are the:

- Council for Trade in Goods — Committees of this Council include Market Access — Agriculture, Sanitary and Phytosanitary Measures, Technical Barriers to Trade, Subsidies and Countervailing Measures, Anti-Dumping Practices, Customs Valuation, Rules of Origin, Import Licensing, Trade-Related Investment Measures, Safeguards.
- Council for Trade-Related Aspects of Intellectual Property Rights
- Council for Trade in Services — Committees of this Council are Trade in Financial Services and Specific Commitments.
- Committees on Trade and Environment, Trade and Development, Regional Trade Agreements, Balance of Payments Restrictions, Budget, Finance and Administration.

The WTO Secretariat is headed by a director-general and does not have branch offices outside Geneva. Since the members make decisions on treaty acceptance, the Secretariat does not have the decision-making role that other international bureaucracies are given. Its role is mainly technical and legal support.

The first Ministerial Conference in Singapore in 1996 added three new working groups to this structure, reporting directly to the General Council:
- The Relationship between Trade and Investment
- The Interaction between Trade and Competition Policy
- The Transparency in Government Procurement

Debate Surrounding National Sovereignty

The World Trade Organization has been the target of much controversy. Demonstrations and threats of violence have plagued several recent trade negotiations by several groups attempting to sway the WTO agenda. These groups feel that the WTO dictates policy, causing member countries essentially to abdicate their national sovereignty on many issues. Critics of the WTO also believe that the WTO promotes commercial interests above all others including the needs of developing area, public health and safety, the environment, and the workforce. Furthermore, it is suggested that the WTO forces developing countries into the WTO but provides little return for the investment of time, money, and trade resources.

When GATT originally was established, it provided a forum for the industrialized countries to negotiate reciprocal tariff reductions. In the last decade, world trading rules have begun to affect areas formerly considered the domain of national governments, such as environmental and public health regulations. In some cases, domestic laws designed to protect the environment or public health have been challenged as potential barriers to trade. This push to reduce all trade barriers has shown the vast differences in national labor and environmental protection legislation. Problems with the WTO arise because its rules are seen as too intrusive by some and because of the lack of specificity of WTO rules in such crucial areas as labor rights. Below is a list of some examples cited by Trade Watch (http://www.tradewatch.org/Shell_Game/Wto.htm), a civil watchdog group, as examples where these problems exist.
- The WTO Agreement on Sanitary and Phytosanitary Measures established a standard for health and safety regulations. In the interests of free trade, governments cannot keep a product out of its market as a public health, safety, or environmental precaution. The government must prove that the product actually poses a significant

threat. This reverses the approach typically taken to public health protection by federal agencies that require products to be proven safe before they are placed on the market.

- The WTO Agreement on Technical Barriers to Trade sets rules on what are called process and production methods (PPMs). These rules state a government cannot take into account the way that a product is made when deciding whether to allow its importation. This means the following cannot be denied access: foreign made goods or services made with child labor, commodities harvested or fished in what a country may deem as cruel or destructive manner, or natural resources extracted in what a country may deem as an environmentally unsound manner.

- The WTO prohibitions on Trade Related Investment Measures (TRIMS) require all WTO-member governments regardless of their level of development to eliminate certain policies that impose conditions on foreign investment. The TRIMs eliminates requirements that foreign investors use local materials or suppliers when doing business in developing countries that would benefit from local capital accumulation.

- The WTO agreement on Trade Related Intellectual Property Measures (TRIPS) forces all countries — rich and poor — to adopt the same, strict guidelines on respecting corporate patents, trade-marks and copyrights. The TRIPs guarantees monopoly ownership over patents.

- The WTO Agreement on Government Procurement (AGP) prevents those governments that signed on from taking into account the behavior of foreign companies when awarding public contracts. This means that governments that have signed the agreement cannot hold foreign corporations accountable for misconduct when awarding lucrative public or government contracts. The AGP is a plurilateral agreement, meaning that unlike the agreements cited above, adoption is voluntary.

TradeWatch, an established trade watchdog group, also recently cited laws or regulations within the last two years in the United States and Europe which have come into conflict with the current WTO standards. Based on these and other instances, TradeWatch claims the WTO's rulings and influence are too far-reaching in cases of national sovereignty, especially in regards to the environment.

General Agreement on Trade in Services (GATS)

In 1999, the value of cross-border trade in services amounted to US$1.35 trillion, or about 20% of total cross-border trade. However, this understates the true size of international trade in services, much of which takes place through establishment in the export market, and is not recorded in balance-of-payments statistics. For the past two decades trade in services has grown faster than merchandise trade. The WTO notes the following benefits of liberalizing services:

- Economic performance
  An efficient services infrastructure is a precondition for economic success. Services such as telecommunications, banking, insurance and transport supply strategically important inputs for all sectors, goods and services. Without the spur of competition, service providers are unlikely to excel in this role — to the detriment of overall economic efficiency and growth. An increasing number of governments thus rely on an open and transparent environment for the provision of services.

- Development
  Access to world-class services helps exporters and producers in developing countries to capitalize on their competitive strength, whatever the goods and services they are selling. A number of developing countries have also been able, building on foreign investment and expertise, to advance in international services markets — from tourism and construction to software development and health care. Services liberalization has thus become a key element of many development strategies.

- Consumer savings
  There is strong evidence in many services that liberalization leads to lower prices, better quality and wider choice for consumers. Such benefits, in turn, work their way through the economic system and help to improve supply conditions for many other products. Thus, even if some prices rise during liberalization — for example, the cost of local calls — price reductions and quality gains elsewhere

will outweigh these sectional cost increase. Moreover, governments remain perfectly able under the GATS, even in a fully liberalized environment, to apply universal-service obligations and to provide for measures that ensure the ability to maintain national security and to assure adequate government revenues.

- Faster innovation
Countries with liberalized services markets have seen greater product and process innovation. The explosive growth of the Internet in the United States is in marked contrast to its slower take-off in many continental European countries that have been more hesitant to embrace telecom reform. Similar contrasts can be drawn in financial services and information technology.

- Greater transparency and predictability
A country's commitments in its WTO services schedule amount to a legally binding guarantee that foreign firms will be allowed to supply their services under stable conditions. This gives everyone with a stake in the sector — producers, investors, workers and users — a clear idea of the rules of the game. They are able to plan for the future with greater certainty, which encourages long-term investment.

- Technology transfer
Services commitments at the WTO help to encourage foreign direct investment (FDI). Such FDI typically brings with it new skills and technologies that spill over into the wider economy in various ways. Domestic employees learn the new skills (and teach them to others when they leave the firm). Domestic firms adopt the new techniques. And firms, in other sectors that use services-sector inputs, such as telecommunications and finance, benefit as well.

Multilateral Agreement

The **General Agreement on Trade in Services (GATS)** is one of 15 agreements from the Uruguay Round of trade negotiations concluded in 1994 that greatly expanded the 1947 General Agreement on Tariffs and Trade (GATT). GATS is the first multilateral agreement to provide legally enforceable rights to trade in all services. It has built-in agenda for continuous liberalization through continuous negotiations. It is the world's first multinational agreement on investment, since it covers not just cross-boundary trade but every possible service sector in which there is the ability to set up a commercial presence in the export market. This includes all the ways in which to provide an international service: cross-border supply, consumption abroad, commercial presence, and presence of natural persons.

There are two exceptions: 1) Article I (3) excludes "services supplied in the exercise of governmental authority". These are services that are supplied neither on a commercial basis nor in competition with other suppliers. 2) The Annex on Air Transport Services exempts from coverage measures affecting air traffic rights and services directly related to the exercise of those rights.

GATS contains four sections:
- The main text containing general principles and obligations
- Annexes dealing with rules for specific sectors
- Specific commitments of individual countries to provide access to their markets
- Lists showing where countries are temporarily not applying the "most-favored-nation" principle of non-discrimination.

Principles of Non-Discrimination

Under GATS, countries cannot discriminate between their trading partners. This principle is known as most-favored-nation (MFN) treatment. Some exceptions are allowed in services. Countries may, in limited circumstances, discriminate, but only under strict conditions. These conditions are listed in each country's schedule of commitments. National treatment applies once a service has entered the market. This means that once a foreign service provider establishes a presence in the market, the member country guarantees it equal standing as domestic service providers under the Law. GATS also requires transparency. Governments must publish all relevant laws and regulations and set up inquiry points within their bureaucracies for foreign companies and governments to use to obtain information about regulations in any service sector. The WTO must also be notified of any changes in regulations that apply to the services that come under specific commitments.

Commitment to Continued Liberalization

GATS requires more negotiations in order to further the liberalization process by increasing the level of commitments in schedules. In services, the Uruguay Round was the first step in a longer-term process of multilateral trade liberalization in the services arena. In the years since the inception of GATS, the economic importance of trade in services has risen.

GATS has three sections regarding its continued commitment to liberalization that set a built-in agenda for continued negotiations. The first section details the process and timeframe for 'Negotiation of Specific Commitments.' Member countries have five years from the signing date to have begun their negotiations and are required to then periodically review their specific commitments thereafter. Considerations for the level of development must be given when dealing with developing nations. The Council for Trade in Services assessed trade in services in overall and sectorally.

The second agenda item is for member countries to create a **schedule of specific commitments** and to work progressively on them. The third item is the **modification procedures** for the schedule of commitments. The schedule of commitments allows each member country to acknowledge the unique and ever-changing nature of its services. It also allows for those commitments that are no longer applicable to be removed.

Agreement on Financial Services

The **Annex on Financial Services** in GATS indicates that governments have the right to take prudential measures, such as those for the protection of investors, depositors and insurance policy holders, and to ensure the integrity and stability of the financial system. It also excludes from the agreement services that are provided when a government exercises its authority over the financial system, for example, services of central banks. Negotiations on specific commitments in financial services continued after the end of the Uruguay Round and were completed in late 1997.

Scope

Similar to GATT, GATS attempts to remove or reduce trade barriers through negotiations of terms and allowances in a universally binding agreement. Article I of the GATS applies to measures affecting trade in services in the following four areas:

AREA	INTERPRETATION
Cross-border services	Services supplied from one country to another
Consumption abroad	Consumers or firms making use of a service in another country
Commercial presence	A foreign company setting up subsidiaries or branches to provide services in another country
	Individuals traveling from their own country to supply services in another

As an interesting side note, some have found that the defined scope in the GATS Article I is somewhat lacking in terms of defining what 'services' means. The GATS defines financial services more specifically later in the document in the Annex, but the broad term of services covers a wide variety of industries with many unique qualities. Some might even be considered both a service and a product which would be dealt with under GATT or a hybrid of both.

According to the Annex on Financial Services, the term financial services includes the following activities:

- Insurance and Insurance-Related Services:
  - Direct insurance (including co-insurance) — life and non-life
  - Reinsurance and retrocession
  - Insurance intermediation, such as brokerage and agency
  - Services auxiliary to insurance, such as consultancy, actuarial, risk assessment and claim settlement

- Banking and Other Financial Services (Excluding Insurance)
  - Acceptance of deposits and other repayable funds from the public

- Lending of all types, including consumer credit, mortgage credit, factoring and financing of commercial transactions
- Financial leasing
- All payment and money transmission services, including credit, charge and debit cards, travelers checks and bankers drafts
- Guarantees and commitments

- Trading for own account or for account of customers, whether on an exchange, in an over-the-counter market or otherwise, the following:
  - Money market instruments (including checks, bills, certificates of deposit)
  - Foreign exchange
  - Derivative products including, but not limited to, futures and options
  - Exchange rate and interest rate instruments, including products such as swaps, forward rate agreements
  - Transferable securities
  - Other negotiable instrument and financial assets, including bullion
- Participation in issues of all kinds of securities, including underwriting and placement as agent (whether publicly or privately) and provision of services related to such issues
- Money brokering
- Asset management, such as cash or portfolio management, all forms of collective investment management, pension fund management, custodial, depository and trust services
- Settlement and clearing services for financial assets, including securities, derivative products, and other negotiable instruments
- Provision and transfer of financial information, and financial data processing and related software by suppliers of other financial services
- Advisory, intermediation and other auxiliary financial services on all the activities listed in subparagraphs (v) through (xv), including credit reference and analysis, investment and portfolio research and advice, advice on acquisitions and on corporate restructuring and strategy

Specific Commitments

Article XX of the GATS sets out the Specific Commitments Schedule for each member country in regards to the commitments outlined in Part III of the agreement. Each schedule outlines the terms and conditions of market access, national treatment, any additional commitments with the timeframe for implementation of those commitments, and the date of entry into force of such commitments. Commitments are undertaken with respect to each of the four different modes of service supply — cross-borde services, consumptionabroad, commercial presence, and persence of natural persons. Most schedules consist of both sectoral and horizontal sections. The horizontal section contains entries that apply across all sectors in the schedule while, the sector-specific section contains entries that apply to a particular service.

Under GATS' Article II, all members are held to two basic obligations of Most Favored Nation treatment and transparency. This Article extends two more specific commitments or obligations: **market access** and **national treatment.** Market access is a negotiated commitment in specified sectors with allowed types of limitations. National treatment implies that a member country does not operate in a fashion benefiting domestic services or service suppliers over foreign competition. The majority of current commitments entered into force on January 1, 1995. The rest are to be phased in by 1997 with the exception being any on-going negotiations.. Participants in extended negotiations have since scheduled new commitments

The Impact of Financial Services Free Trade

Free trade in financial services has several positive effects. Financial services trade encourages the transfer of skills and knowledge, puts downward pressure on costs, and promotes financial innovation. Broader use of more diverse financial instruments, risk diversification across borders, and new skills also promote development and transparency of markets. All other things equal, disruptions arising from financial crises are likely to be less severe in well-developed and internationally open financial systems. Currency exchange markets are likely to remain liquid — reducing the volatility of exchange rates. Open markets with a foundation of good information facilitate switching to foreign sources of capital if necessary.

In the United States, some changes have occurred as a result of the schedule of specific commitment taken by the United States. Some state-level restrictions in relation to the issuance of licenses to non-residents in insurance and services auxiliary to insurance have been lifted. Restrictions have also been lifted in relation to the issuance of branch or agency licenses to foreign banks, as well as some state restrictions on the opening of representative offices by foreign banks. Market access and national treatment are to be provided to foreign firms with respect to interstate banking and interstate branching of banks, except in the case of de novo branching.

The Question of Sovereign Regulation

It is potentially hazardous to allow foreign competition without adequate regulatory and supervisory control. Of the last twenty-five banking crises in the world, eighteen were preceded by financial market liberalization.

Services negotiations do not typically follow the same pattern as classic trade negotiations in which countries exchange concessions in order to get access to each other's markets. In services negotiations, countries are seek different but complementary objectives. The developed countries are seek market access. The developing countries are seeking capital and service market development to help build a competitive infrastructure. Countries will negotiate in their best interests. The coordination of regulation is the major issue. In regulated industries, such as financial services, GATS must achieve a pro-competitive overlay on existing regulations that vary widely in order to assure market access for foreign service suppliers. Market access should not undermine or limit legitimate domestic regulatory objectives. Clearly the safety and soundness of financial institutions or the security of networks is paramount for any country (Lang 2000).

References

Abu-Akeel, A. (1999). Definition of trade in services under GATS: Legal implications. *The George Washington Journal of International Law and Economics*, 32(2), 189–210.

Ahn, D. (2000). Linkages between international financial and trade institutions —
IMF, World Bank and WTO. *Journal of World Trade*, 34(4), 1–36.

Anonymous. (2001). International developments and securities markets. *Norges
Bank Financial Stability*, 1, 9–12.

Anonymous. (2001). The future of globalization of the financial services industry.
Journal of Taxation of Financial Institutions, 14(3), 27, 34.

Anonymous. (2000). Cross-border trade in financial services: Economics and
regulation. *Financial Market Trends*,(72), 23–60.

Barlow, M. (2001). The last frontier. *The Ecologist*, 31(1), 38–42.

Barshefsky, C. (2001). Trade policy for a networked world. *Foreign Affairs*, 80(2),
134–146.

Finger, M. K., & Schuknecht. (1999). Special Studies: Trade Finance and Financial
Crisis, WTO Publications (Geneva, Switzerland).

Kono, M., Low, P., Luanga, M., Mattoo, & others. Special Studies: Opening
Markets in Financial Services and the Role of the GATS, WTO Publications
(Geneva, Switzerland).

Lang, J. M. (2000). The first five years of the WTO: General agreement on trade in
services. *Law and Policy in International Business*, 31(3), 801–809.

Mattoo, A. (2000). Financial services and the WTO: Liberalisation commitments of
the developing and transition economies. *The World Economy*, 23(3), 351–38.

Appendix 3.1
The World Trade Organization Members
(and Date of Membership) as of January 2, 2002

Albania, 8 September 2000
Angola, 23 November 1996
Antigua and Barbuda, 1 January
　1995
Argentina, 1 January 1995
Australia, 1 January 1995
Austria, 1 January 1995
Bahrain, 1 January 1995
Bangladesh, 1 January 1995
Barbados, 1 January 1995
Belgium, 1 January 1995
Belize, 1 January 1995
Benin, 22 February 1996
Bolivia, 12 September 1995
Botswana, 31 May 1995
Brazil, 1 January 1995
Brunei Darussalam, 1 January
　1995
Bulgaria, 1 December 1996
Burkina Faso, 3 June 1995
Burundi, 23 July 1995
Cameroon, 13 December 1995
Canada, 1 January 1995
Central African Republic, 31 May
　1995
Chad, 19 October 1996
Chile, 1 January 1995
China, 11 December 2001
Colombia, 30 April 1995
Congo, 27 March 1997

Costa Rica, 1 January 1995
Côte d'Ivoire, 1 January 1995
Croatia, 30 November 2000
Cuba, 20 April 1995
Cyprus, 30 July 1995
Czech Republic, 1 January 1995
Democratic Republic of the
　Congo, 1 January 1997
Denmark, 1 January 1995
Djibouti, 31 May 1995
Dominica, 1 January 1995
Dominican Republic, 9 March
　1995
Ecuador, 21 January 1996
Egypt, 30 June 1995
El Salvador, 7 May 1995
Estonia, 13 November 1999
European Community, 1 January
　1995
Fiji, 14 January 1996
Finland, 1 January 1995
France, 1 January 1995
Gabon, 1 January 1995
The Gambia, 23 October 1996
Georgia, 14 June 2000
Germany, 1 January 1995
Ghana, 1 January 1995
Greece, 1 January 1995
Grenada, 22 February 1996
Guatemala, 21 July 1995

Guinea Bissau, 31 May 1995
Guinea, 25 October 1995
Guyana, 1 January 1995
Haiti, 30 January 1996
Honduras, 1 January 1995
Hong Kong, China, 1 January 1995
Hungary, 1 January 1995
Iceland, 1 January 1995
India, 1 January 1995
Indonesia, 1 January 1995
Ireland, 1 January 1995
Israel, 21 April 1995
Italy, 1 January 1995
Jamaica, 9 March 1995
Japan, 1 January 1995
Jordan, 11 April 2000
Kenya, 1 January 1995
Korea, Republic of, 1 January 1995
Kuwait, 1 January 1995
Kyrgyz Republic, 20 December 1998
Latvia, 10 February 1999
Lesotho, 31 May 1995
Liechtenstein, 1 September 1995
Lithuania, 31 May 2001
Luxembourg, 1 January 1995
Macao, China, 1 January 1995
Madagascar, 17 November 1995
Malawi, 31 May 1995
Malaysia, 1 January 1995
Maldives, 31 May 1995
Mali, 31 May 1995
Malta, 1 January 1995
Mauritania, 31 May 1995
Mauritius, 1 January 1995
Mexico, 1 January 1995

Moldova, 26 July 2001
Mongolia, 29 January 1997
Morocco, 1 January 1995
Mozambique, 26 August 1995
Myanmar, 1 January 1995
Namibia, 1 January 1995
Netherlands, — For the Kingdom in Europe and for the Netherlands Antilles, 1 January 1995
New Zealand, 1 January 1995
Nicaragua, 3 September 1995
Niger, 13 December 1996
Nigeria, 1 January 1995
Norway, 1 January 1995
Oman, 9 November 2000
Pakistan, 1 January 1995
Panama, 6 September 1997
Papua New Guinea, 9 June 1996
Paraguay, 1 January 1995
Peru, 1 January 1995
Philippines, 1 January 1995
Poland, 1 July 1995
Portugal, 1 January 1995
Qatar, 13 January 1996
Romania, 1 January 1995
Rwanda, 22 May 1996
Saint Kitts and Nevis, 21 February 1996
Saint Lucia, 1 January 1995
Saint Vincent & the Grenadines, 1 January 1995
Senegal, 1 January 1995
Separate Customs Territory of Taiwan, Penghu, Kinmen and Matsu, 1 January 2002
Sierra Leone, 23 July 1995
Singapore, 1 January 1995

Slovak Republic, 1 January 1995
Slovenia, 30 July 1995
Solomon Islands, 26 July 1996
South Africa, 1 January 1995
Spain, 1 January 1995
Sri Lanka, 1 January 1995
Suriname, 1 January 1995
Swaziland, 1 January 1995
Sweden, 1 January 1995
Switzerland, 1 July 1995
Tanzania, 1 January 1995
Thailand, 1 January 1995
Togo, 31 May 1995
Trinidad and Tobago, 1 March
1995

Tunisia, 29 March 1995
Turkey, 26 March 1995
Uganda, 1 January 1995
United Arab Emirates, 10 April
1996
United Kingdom, 1 January 1995
United States of America,
1 January 1995
Uruguay, 1 January 1995
Venezuela, 1 January 1995
Zambia, 1 January 1995
Zimbabwe, 5 March 1995

Chapter 4

Asian Pacific Economic Cooperation

Introduction

A region is a group of countries with marked interdependence across dimensions. This pattern of interdependence is often indicated by patterns of economic and political transactions and social communications. The manifestations are more than the flow of goods and people, but are also include social and cognitive constructs that are rooted in political practice. The effects of international environment on regions can lead to a relatively open (as in the 1990s) or closed (as in the 1930s) type of regionalism. Regions can be peaceful and rich, or war-prone and poor. Regions can (1) experience processes of enlargement and set standards for a growing number of governments, or (2) suffer from retraction from the world economy. When exploring regionalism in Asia, it is important to see the regional trading blocs as larger than economic devices alone.

Asian Pacific Economic Cooperation (APEC)

APEC is an organization established to mitigate the economic block and trade protection trend prevailing in the 1980s and to promote increased trade liberalization while adhering to GATT. The goal was to promote economic cooperation and integration in the Pacific region. The United States was a driving force in the creation of APEC because the United States considered APEC to be a means of securing the strategic position of the United States in the region. Established at a meeting held in November 1989 at Canberra, Australia, APEC's mission was to configure an open economic alliance in the Asia-Pacific region. Through continued negotiations, APEC has emerged as the major regional consulting entity in the Asian-Pacific rim. APEC, now composed of 21 economies with differing backgrounds, interests and political systems, helps maintain stability in the region by facilitating a dialogue among its members.

Origins and Membership of APEC

APEC was established in response to the growing interdependence among Asia-Pacific economies to advance Asia-Pacific economic dynamism and sense of community. APEC was created as a ministerial-level organization, operated by consensus. Members conduct their activities and work programs on the basis of open dialogue with equal respect for the views of all participants. There were 12 founding members:

Australia
Brunei Darussalam
Canada
Indonesia
Japan
Republic of Korea
Malaysia
New Zealand
Republic of the Philippines
Singapore
Thailand
Unites States

Since 1989, nine APEC has added nine additional members.

Country	DATE OF EFFECTIVE MEMBERSHIP (November)
People's Republic of China	1991
Hong Kong (Hong Kong, China since July (1997)	1991
Chinese Taipei (Taiwan)	1991
Mexico	1993
Papua New Guinea	1993
Chile	1994
Peru	1998
Russia	1998
Vietnam	1998

In September 1992, the 4th APEC Ministerial Meeting agreed to set up a secretariat as a supporting mechanism and accepted the offer from Singapore to host the Secretariat. The Secretariat was officially established on February 12, 1993 in Singapore. The Secretariat has two-categories of staff: 1) Professional Staff Members (PSMs) that are seconded from the government of member economies, and 2) Supportive Staff Members (SSMs).

The APEC Chair rotates annually among APEC members. As Chair, that member is responsible for hosting the annual ministerial meeting of foreign and economic ministers. There are three observers of APEC: Secretariat, Pacific Economic Cooperation Council (PECC), Pacific Islands Forum Secretariat (PIF), and Association of Southeast Asian Nations (ASEAN).

The PECC is a non-governmental organization with the goal of promoting economic cooperation in the Pacific Rim. Government officials, academics, and business people work together to develop answers to regional economic problems. Founded in 1980, PECC is the only private-sector observer in the ministerial forum of APEC.

The PECC Secretariat is also based in Singapore. Members of PECC include 23 economies, two associate members, and two institutional members.

Member Economies:
Australia
Brunei Darussalam
Canada
Chile
China
Colombia
Ecuador
Hong Kong, China
Indonesia
Japan
Korea
Malaysia
Mexico
New Zealand
Peru

The Philippines
Russia
Singapore
Pacific Islands Forum
Chinese Taipei
Thailand
The United States
Vietnam

Associate Members:
France (Pacific Territories)
Mongolia

Institutional Members:
Pacific Trade and Development Conference (PAFTAD)
Pacific Basin Economic Council (PBEC)

Pacific Economic Cooperation Council (PECC)

PECC establishes task forces and working groups to concentrate on specific policy areas. These groups organize seminars and workshops, conduct studies, and publish the conclusions and recommendations for the benefit of the Pacific community. The areas that the task forces address are:
- Capital and financial markets
- Fisheries development
- Pacific island nations
- Science and technology

Pacific Island Forum (PIF)

The PIF represents heads of government of all the independent and self-governing Pacific Island countries, Australia, and New Zealand. Since 1971, when it was founded, the Forum enables the members to express political views and to cooperate in areas of political and economic concern. The Secretariat of PIF is in Suva, Fiji. Member countries are:

Australia
Cook Islands

Federated States of Micronesia
Fiji
Kiribati
Nauru
New Zealand
Niue
Palau
Papua New Guinea
Republic of the Marshall Islands
Samoa
Solomon Islands
Tonga
Tuvalu
Vanuatu

Association of Southeast Asian Nations (ASEAN)

The ASEAN Declaration of 1967 exhorts the association to attain its economic, social and cultural aims through "joint endeavors" and "active collaboration and mutual assistance." Yet, it does not call for the ASEAN member states to take common political positions. ASEAN, as more tightly drawn body whose members seem to have more in common with one another, has difficulty in setting a uniform tariff reduction policy. The ASEAN Declaration states that the aims and purposes of the Association are:

- To accelerate the economic growth, social progress and cultural development in the region through joint endeavors in the spirit of equality and partnership.
- To strengthen the foundation for a prosperous and peaceful community of Southeast Asian nations.
- To promote regional peace and stability through abiding respect for justice and the rule of law in the relationship among countries in the region.
- To adhere to the principles of the United Nations Charter.

ASEAN member countries are:
Brunei
Laos

Malaysia
The Philippines
Thailand
Cambodia
Indonesia
Myanmar
Singapore
Vietnam

The Outcomes of Past Intergovernmental Meetings of APEC

Blake Island, Washington State, US, 1993

On November 20, 1993, the leaders of the member economies met at Blake Island, Seattle, Washington upon the invitation of the United States. The main objective was to discuss major issues in the APEC region. This gathering of economic leaders arguably has become the single most important institution in the Asia Pacific region. It brought attention to APEC's vision of free trade and investment — as a forum for leaders to meet on a regular basis both as a group and bilaterally to discuss current issues and resolve disputes. The vision was to harness the energy of its diverse economies, strengthen cooperation, and promote prosperity, continue in the spirit of openness, and deepen the partnership, continue dynamic growth, and contribute to an expanding world economy by supporting an open international trading system.

APEC sought:

- *To reduce trade and investment barriers so that trade expands within the region and with the world.*
- *To allow goods, services, capital, and investment to flow freely among APEC economies.*
- *To enable people in APEC economies to share the benefits of economic growth through higher incomes, high-skilled and high-paying jobs, and increased mobility.*

In addition to efforts to reduce these barriers, several non-trade issues were to be addressed. These included facilitating improved education and training that would produce rising literacy rates, provide the skills for maintaining economic growth, and encourage the sharing of ideas that contribute to the arts and sciences. Advances in telecommunications would eventually shrink the time and distance barriers in the region and link APEC economies so that goods and people move quickly and efficiently.

The APEC economies also sought to improve the environment — protect the quality of air, water, and green spaces, manage energy sources and renewable resources to ensure sustainable growth, and provide a more secure future.

Bogor, Indonesia, 1994

The outcome of this meeting was the Declaration of Common Resolve stipulating the mutual commitment to achieve free and open trade and investment in the region no later than 2010 for the industrialized economies and 2020 for developing economies

Osaka, Japan, 1995

On November 19, 1995 in Osaka Japan, an Action Plan was created. The Osaka Action Agenda addressed trade and investment liberalization and facilitation in PART I. In Part II, the Action Plan stressed economic and technical cooperation in areas such as energy and transportation, infrastructure, small and medium enterprises, and agricultural technology in Part II.

Manila, The Philippines, 1996

The Manila Action Plan for APEC (MAPA), established on November 25, 1996, included individual and collective action plans and progress reports, in recognition of the Bogor goals of open trade and investment by 2010 for industrialized economies and 2020 for developing economies. The Information Technology Agreement of Part II of the Osaka Action Agenda was also endorsed. The MAPA instructed ministers (1) to identify sectors in which early voluntary liberalization would have a positive impact on trade, investment, and economic growth in individual member economies and regionally and (2) to submit recommendations on how this could be achieved. The goals of the Action Plan:

* *Simplify customs clearance procedures*
* *Implement effective intellectual property rights commitments*

- *Harmonize custom valuation*
- *Facilitate comprehensive trade in services*
- *Enhance the environment for investment*

APEC economic leaders instructed the ministers of APEC to give high priority to the following six themes in economic and technical cooperation:
- *Develop human capital*
- *Foster safe and efficient capital markets*
- *Strengthen economic infrastructure*
- *Harness technologies of the future*
- *Promote environmentally sustainable growth*
- *Encourage the growth of small and medium-sized enterprises*

Vancouver, Canada, 1997

In Vancouver, Canada in November 1997, the participants discussed regional financial developments. They especially noted that the economies and the international community were very interested in restoration of financial stability and healthy and in sustainable growth in response to recent instability. This led the members to urge rapid implementation of the Manila Framework.

Three pillars of international economic cooperation were established:
- *Trade and investment liberalization*
- *Business facilitation*
- *Economic and technical cooperation*

Fifteen early voluntary liberalization sectors endorsed with nine to be advanced throughout 1998 with plans to implementation beginning in 1999. The nine "priority" sectors were chemicals, fish products, forestry products, energy goods and services, environmental goods and services, gems and jewelry, medical equipment, telecommunications, and toys. The six "non-priority" sectors were automotive standards, aircraft, fertilizer, food, oilseeds, and rubber.

It was agreed that electronic commerce is the most important technological breakthrough of the decade and groundwork was laid to develop a program on electronic commerce in the region. Improved financial capital market access was noted as necessary for the development of regional infrastructure with recognition of the importance of private sector participation. The leaders called for collaboration with multilateral financial institutions and the private sector in order to develop domestic capital markets. In this regard, the specific requests were to continue work to:

- *Involve private sector financiers and providers of risk coverage.*
- *Focus on investment ratings to promote the development of robust and liquid domestic bond markets.*
- *Include markets for asset-backed securities to enhance private investment in large-scale infrastructure projects.*

Kuala Lumpur, Malaysia, 1998

In Kuala Lumpur on November 17 and 18, 1998, APEC reaffirmed their confidence in the strong economic fundamentals and prospects for recovery for the economies of the Asia-Pacific. Member economies agreed to pursue a cooperative growth strategy to end the financial crisis; and to strengthen social safety nets, financial systems, trade and investment flows, the scientific and technological base, human resources development, economic infrastructure, and business and commercial links. The objective was to provide the base, and to set the pace for sustained growth. The private sector could be involved in the revitalization of these goals by:

- *Addressing companies' heavy debt burdens.*
- *Restoring access to trade and working capital financing as critical to achieving renewed economic growth in those economies most affected by the economic crisis.*
- *Mobilizing assistance to implement an accelerated financial and corporate sector restructuring through use of multilateral development bank guarantees and other mechanisms.*
- *Increasing the availability of working capital and trade finance through cooperative efforts (1) between export credit and insurance agencies and (2) between bilateral institutions and the multilateral development banks.*
- *Supporting efforts to mobilize significant private sector equity capital and investment to help companies and financial institutions successfully restructure finances and operations in the region.*
- *Reviewing and removing regulatory and legal impediments hindering the ability of private financial institutions to participate actively in*

the restructuring of the private sector debts, while encouraging export credit and insurance agencies to play an active role in encouraging restructuring.

- *Encouraging the multilateral development banks to use new financial instruments to help foster and leverage private sector capital flows.*
- *Strengthening domestic financial systems to withstand the potentially destabilizing short-term flows and to ensure the allocation of long-term capital to productive uses.*

Auckland, New Zealand, 1999

In Auckland, New Zealand (September 1999), the leaders supported a consensus to ensure that reforms of the international financial system and domestic financial markets were mutually reinforcing. APEC leaders advocated greater transparency and openness including improved reliability and timeliness of information and clearer accountability for decisions and judgments in both the public and private sectors.

Meetings of Finance Ministers of APEC

The finance ministers of APEC also have met yearly to address issues of financial infrastructure and market operations. The eighth meeting in Suzhou, People's Republic of China was held in September 2001. At this meeting, financial ministers identified the following as critical needs in the APEC region:

- *Further strengthening of the bank regulation and supervision*
- *Continuing development of skills of banking, securities and insurance regulation*
- *Further trade and investment liberalization to increase investor confidence, attract capital to the region, stimulate growth, and reduce poverty*
- *Strengthening the transparency and disclosure standards for financial market participants*
- *Promoting financial stability and crisis prevention*
- *Addressing the issues surrounding electronic marketing and delivery of financial services and electronic payment and settlement of financial transactions*

The Finance Ministers concluded that APEC had demonstrated the vulnerability of many of the members' economies and agreed to launch a new program on Finance and Development. This initiative is aimed at strengthening capacity in the APEC region especially in the areas of finance and economic development.

Slower Development of Binding Agreements

It has been noted that APEC has resisted legalization of its processes and obligations, leading to few tangible results. Because member economies have differing economic status, tensions have arisen within APEC. The diverse perspectives of the participants in the financial ministers' talks are often difficult to reconcile. While talks will continue, many economies are do not have a clear and detailed strategy on how to combat global slowdown or to have a greater impact on the world economy.

At a recent meeting of finance ministers, Kim Hak-Su, Executive Secretary of the Economic and Social Commission for Asia and the Pacific (ESCAP), told the meeting that the Asian economic crisis of the mid-1990s had amply demonstrated that participation in global markets was by no means a smooth or equitable process. The more industrialized East Asian economies had almost fully integrated into the world economy and had benefited enormously from globalization but that countries in less-developed areas had experienced a more mixed outcome. These less-developed nations, Pacific island countries, and economies in transition remained marginalized in their ability to influence despite substantial increases in intra-regional trade flows.

Other attendees committed as follows:

- Chinese Vice Minister of Finance Jin Liqun: "China is doing its own homework to maintain domestic demand, but I don't think you should expect China to play such a big role as the United States or even Japan."
- Singapore Finance Minister Richard Hu: "All the major economies should contribute."
- Japanese Finance Minister Masajuro Shiokawa: "We are committed to carrying out reforms."

These statements help to illustrate the different perspectives of APEC members.

Responding to the Asian Financial Crisis

Asia's financial crisis came unannounced and was largely unanticipated. In 1996, the region saw itself well poised to extend its success into the twenty-first century. In a 1997 press conference, IMF Managing Director Michel Camdessus remarked that the global economic outlook warranted "rational exuberance." At its spring 1997 meeting, the Interim Committee of the International Monetary Fund (IMF) approved a plan to amend the Articles of Agreement to extend the IMF's jurisdiction to cover the movement of capital.

The role of APEC in dealing with the crisis has been strictly limited. The lack of formalized institutional structures has meant that Southeast Asia has had to depend heavily on bilateral relations and initiatives to solve problems. The extent to which the regional economies have come to the direct assistance of the crisis-hit economies in Southeast Asia has been low. Japan contributed the most to recovery.

Japan continues a pro-active approach in responding to the Southeast Asian crisis as a result of redefining itself. Japan has made significant efforts to redefine its identity. This redefinition has compelled Japan to engage more actively the larger East Asia and has increased its self-assurance making, Japan more willing to take initiatives in political, security and economic areas.

The Japanese government proposed an "Asian Monetary Fund" (AMF) in August 1997 with the aim to provide a pool of available funds that could be quickly disbursed to alleviate selling pressure of the regional currencies. In addition, the AMF would provide emergency balance of payments support for the economies in crisis. The AMF was enthusiastically welcomed by most East Asian economies. It is important to note that Japan has been the largest single-country contributor to the IMF-orchestrated financial assistance packages to the Southeast Asian economies. The United States, however, contributed only $3 billion to Indonesia directly with this sum being heavily tied to the IMF conditions.

At the Fifth APEC Summit in November 1997 in Vancouver, the APEC leaders endorsed and called for a quick implementation of the Manila Framework for Enhanced Asian Regional Cooperation to Promote Financial Stability. The Framework included the following initiatives:

- *A cooperative financing arrangement that would supplement IMF resources*
- *Enhanced economic and technical cooperation, particularly in strengthening domestic financial systems and regulatory capacities*
- *A mechanism for regional surveillance to complement the IMF's global surveillance*

The ASEAN finance ministers endorsed the idea of a regional surveillance process in Manila in November 1997 to complement and supplement the IMF's global surveillance role. The ASEAN Surveillance Process was initially uaccountable to the Asian Development Bank (ADB), but recently transferred to the ASEAN Secretariat in Jakarta. The overall objectives of the Surveillance Process are broadly to assist ASEAN members in spotting a potential crisis and responding to it accordingly by:

- *Assessing the vulnerability of ASEAN members to financial disruptions and crises.*
- *Improving the coordination of ASEAN members' economic policies through the dissemination of sound practices that meet international standards.*
- *Promoting a 'peer monitoring' environment among ASEAN members through a review of potentially vulnerable sectors.*

A possible constraint on the potential effectiveness of the Surveillance Process is the actual political power of ASEAN. Substantial asymmetries in the sizes and the levels of economic development of member nations, on the one hand, and the ASEAN policy of strict non-intervention in one another's affairs (economic and political), on the other, may make it extremely difficult to operate a regional surveillance mechanism effectively. It is unclear whether the inclusion of a larger grouping like APEC will help ease some of these asymmetries, escalate it, or have little effect.

Another potential impediment to a well functioning surveillance mechanism is the lack of transparency in economic data and general public documentation of economic and financial activities in the region. It appears that authorities in the region have not always been forthcoming about their economic and financial situations and have used economic data as a strategic tool rather than a public good. The need to establish benchmarks for timely and accurate data is critical. Foreign investors and lenders must be able to make rational and economically viable decisions with reasonably accurate perceptions of risks and benefits.

The Hanoi Plan

The Hanoi Plan is the first in a series of plans of action leading to the actualization of ASEAN Vision 2020, adopted in the Second ASEAN Informal Summit (December 1997). The Hanoi Plan has a six-year time frame and will be reviewed every three years coinciding with the ASEAN Summit Meetings. While the ASEAN leaders have touted the Hanoi Plan as a bold plan, there are few implementation guidelines. The Hanoi Plan of Action was adopted at the Sixth ASEAN Summit. In addition to promoting social development and addressing the social impact of the financial and economic crisis, the plan called for the following:

* *Strengthening of macroeconomic and financial cooperation*
* *Enhancing economic integration through measures such as the acceleration of the implementation of the Asian Framework Agreement (AfrA) as part of the Hanoi Plan.*
* *Promoting science and technology development and developing information technology infrastructure*
* *Protecting the environment and promoting sustainable development*
* *Strengthening regional peace and security*
* *Enhancing ASEAN's role as an effective force for peace, justice, and moderation in the Asia-Pacific and the world*
* *Promoting ASEAN awareness and its standing in the international community*
* *Improving ASEAN's structures and mechanisms*

The Keys to Financial Integration in Asia

Recent activity that should have a major impact in the area of financial services opportunity includes meetings aimed at working on aspects of economic interdependence and the strengthening of the financial architecture of the region. Recently, the Institute for International Monetary Affairs, the International Monetary Fund, and the World Bank were joint sponsors of a conference, "Economic Interdependence Shaping Asia-Pacific in the 21st Century" focused on three aspects of regional interaction:

- *Trade and investment linkages*
- *Financial market integration and capital flows*
- *Managing macroeconomic interdependence and spillovers through strengthening the regional financial architecture*

The conference included the presentation of new analytic work on the region's economies, panel discussions featuring regional experts, and an exchange of ideas and views. Discussion focused on the growing economic interdependence that has been a defining feature of the Asia-Pacific region. As highlighted by the financial crisis, many economies in the region are highly integrated with the global economic and financial system or are in the process of becoming integrated. This has led to questions about the role of regional policy coordination as a compliment to global reforms.

References

Anonymous. (1999). APEC ups ante on free trade. *Business Asia*, 7(14), 2.

Anonymous. (2000). General agreement on trade in services. *The Oil and Gas Journal*, 98(19), 9.

Anonymous. (1999). APEC adopts electronic commerce models. *Computer Dealer News*, 15(43), 23.

Anonymous. (1999). Siew welcomes WTO invitation; stresses national sovereignty. *China News*, 475.

Anonymous. (1998). Electronic commerce and the APEC. *Business America*, 119(1), 19.

Anonymous. (1999). Asian capital markets: Help wanted? *The Economist* (US), 351(8120), 85.

Collins, K. (2000). International accounting rate reform: The role of international organizations and implications for developing countries. *Law and Policy in International Business*, 31(3), 1077.

Delahunty, J. (1999). APEC At Auckland. *Monthly Review*, 51(7), 15.

Evans, P. M. (2001). Cooperative security and its discontents in Asia Pacific: The ASEAN connection. *American Asian Review*, 19(2), 99–119.

Freeman, P. (1997). Vietnam trade luring few takers. *Puget Sound Business Journal*, 18(26), 38.

Gazel, R. C., & Lamb, R. L. (1998). Will the tenth district catch the Asian flu? *Economic Review - Federal Reserve Bank of Kansas City*, 83(2), 9–26.

Katzenstein, P.J. (2000). Regionalism and Asia. *New Political Economy*, 5(3), 353–368.

Linarelli, J. (2000). The role of dispute settlement in world trade law: Some lessons from the Kodak-Fuji dispute. *Law and Policy in International Business*, 31(2), 263.

Ravulur, N. (1997). APEC likely to admit Russia in a few years. *Puget Sound Business Journal*, 18(26), 37+.

Sorin, A. T., & Burton, Z. (2001). The effects of the Asian crisis on global equity markets. *The Financial Review*, 36(1), 125–140.

Stokes, B. (1999). Economic interests: It's all about power. *National Journal*, 3392.

Wesley, M. (1999). The Asian crisis and the adequacy of regional institutions. *Contemporary Southeast Asia*, 21(1), 54–73.

Wilhelm, S. (1999). Song plays solo on APEC panel. *Puget Sound Business Journal*, 20(23), 21.

Wolcott, J. (1997). Japan trade crisis imperiled local business. *Puget Sound Business Journal*, 18(26), 39+.

Yonan, A. Jr. (2000). Capital Flows to Emerging Markets to Rise 30%. *Wall Street Journal(E)* A2.

Chapter 5

Free Trade Area of The Americas

Introduction

Before the North American Free Trade Agreement (NAFTA) was enacted with the United States, Canada, and Mexico as signatories, a number of major trade agreements were effected in Latin America:

- *The Latin American Free Trade Area — LAFTA (replaced by the Latin American Integration Association — LAIA)*
- *The Central American Common Market — CACM*
- *The Caribbean Free Trade Association — CARIFTA (replaced by the Caribbean Community — CARICOM)*
- *The Andean Group*
- *Mercado Común del Sur — Mercosur*
- *The Group of Three.*

Currently, the most comprehensive of these in terms of countries represented is the Free Trade Area of the Americas.

Latin American Regional Pacts

Latin American Free Trade Area/ Latin American Integration Association

Formed in 1960, the Latin American Free Trade Area (LAFTA) originally had, its main objective, the gradual elimination of trade barriers and the progressive reduction of tariffs affecting trade flows. Member countries included (and year of membership if not 1960) were:

Argentina
Brazil
Chile
Ecuador
Mexico
Paraguay
Peru
Uruguay
Bolivia (1966)
Venezuela (1967)

The goal was to accomplish this liberalization in a 12-year transition period of continuous multilateral negotiations. The actual process was to use a product-by-product strategy following GATT-type principles of Most Favored Nation (MFN) treatment and reciprocity, while granting more favorable consideration for the least developed countries of Bolivia and Ecuador. Negotiations centered around national lists of products for which each country individually agreed to reduce tariffs by at least 8% per year with annual negotiations and common lists of products for which all countries must have reduced tariffs to zero and must have eliminated all quantitative restrictions by the end of the transition period with negotiations every three years. Ultimately, seventy-five percent of all trade was expected to be covered under such provisions by 1972. The products contained on the national lists more than doubled from 1962 to 1968 before progress stalled. Only one common list was ever approved but it never became effective.

The failure of LAFTA stems from a lack of diversity in the products traded intra-regionally. Since most were basic primary products, the concept of comparative advantage was difficult to establish. In addition, there was relative macroeconomic instability in Argentina and Brazil, two of the major members of the group. The reactions to the lack of progress in LAFTA led to the formation of a subgroup (the Andean Group in 1969) and replacement of the organization by the Latin American Integration Association (LAIA) in 1980.

LAIA did not seek to establish a free trade area within Latin America, but sought instead to facilitate the formation of bilateral commercial agreements that could later include other countries in the region. The basic approach of LAIA is bilateral tariff negotiations that later can be extended to other countries, with no predetermined schedule and no intent to establish a common external tariff for the region. That is, there is no stated intent to become a customs union. (See Chapter 1 — Stages of Regional Integration.) LAIA was based on the principles of pluralism, convergence, flexibility, and differential treatments on the basis of the economic development of countries — to make possible various forms of agreements between member countries.

Central American Common Market

In contrast to LAIA, the Central American Common Market is a much smaller group consisting of five countries — Guatemala, El Salvador, Honduras, Nicaragua, and Panama (member as of 1993). This is a much smaller region, with less economic activity as compared to LAIA.

The first steps to regional integration in Central America were bilateral trade agreements among the five countries of the region during the 1950s. By 1960, this arrangement had evolved into a full-fledged common market, the CACM. The treaty included an immediate adoption of free trade within the region for most manufacturing commodities and a regional payments mechanism administered by the Central American Clearing House. By 1966, more than 94% of the items of the CACM tariff classification were subject to free trade within the CACM and a common external tariff for goods from outside the CACM. These successes of the CACM have been attributed at least partially to relative inability of the small domestic import sectors to effectively resist the initiatives of the CACM.

Caribbean Free Trade Association/ Caribbean Community

In 1965, the year of its formation, the Caribbean Free Trade Association (CARIFTA) immediately freed imports and exports within the region from duties and non-tariff barriers. There was a five-year transition period for those few products that the member countries previously had designated for import substitution treatment. Unlike the Central American agreement, CARIFTA did not establish a common external tariff for goods from outside the region. However, the benefits of the arrangement accrued primarily to the more economically advanced members of the group. The less developed members advocated changes that would be of more benefit to them.

The member countries and their dates of membership (other than 1965) are:

Antiqua
Barbadoes
Guyana
Jamaica (1968)
Trinidad & Tobago (1968)
Grenada (1968)
Dominica (1968)
St. Lucia (1968)
St. Vincent (1968)
St. Kitts & Nevis (1968)
Belize (1971)

In 1973, CARIFTA was replaced by the Caribbean Community (CARICOM). The objectives of the new Caribbean group included the unification of monetary and fiscal policies, as well as commercial activity. Planning agencies for agricultural and industrial development were created. A common external tariff for goods from outside the region was instituted. The objectives of CARICOM included:

- *Strengthening coordination and regulation of the economic and trade relations among member countries.*
- *Sustained expansion and continuing integration of economic activities.*
- *Achievement of a greater measure of economic independence and effectiveness of its member countries in collective bargaining situations.*
- *Coordination of foreign policies and functional cooperation.*

The difficulties of integrating the economies of countries with different relative sizes remained, however, as did the problems associated with a lack of diversity of production capabilities among the members.

The Andean Group

The Andean Group represents a much larger population than either CACM or CARICOM. As a spin-off of LAFTA, the Andean Group was formed in 1969 with the expressed purpose of avoiding the problems experienced by the larger Latin American group, while pursuing import substitution and keeping out investment by foreign multinationals. It was felt that a comprehensive coordination of industrial planning would be necessary to accomplish these goals. The main objectives of the Andean Group were liberalization of regional trade, gradual achievement of a common external tariff, establishing strategic regional investment programs that would offset the costs of the integration process for specific members, and instituting a common code for foreign direct investment. Members of the Andean Group (and year of membership if not 1969) are:[8]

Bolivia
Columbia
Ecuador
Peru
Venezuela (1973)

In the agreement between the signatories of the Andean Group, a provision was made for the **harmonization of financial services**. The General Secretariat of the Andean Group was to propose a Project of Decision containing the standards that regulate the process of liberalization of trade in financial services among the member countries.

Despite the ambitious goals of the group, the results were not as dramatic as had been anticipated. As of 1980, over 25% of the items subject to tariff had not begun the liberalization process. By 1985, only three of the eight strategic regional investment programs had been approved. The reasons for the less-than-anticipated results were a large number of product exemptions from the tariff liberalization plan, no agreement on the common external tariff, and the inconsistency of regional industrial strategy vs. the strategies of individual member countries.

A Shift in Focus

It appears that early lackluster results of LAFTA, CARIFTA, and the Andean Group are tied directly to the common emphasis on regional import substitution in the face of individual economic systems that did not

---

[8] Chile was one of the founding members of the Andean Group but left the group in 1976.

adequately complement each other. The debt crisis of the 1980s sharply underscored the fallacy of this inward focus. While Asian developing countries with a strong, outward, export-oriented focus grew rapidly, the Latin American economies suffered. These realities have pushed Latin American countries into a more aggressive stance in favor of export-oriented policies.

In 1990, the Andean Group was relaunched with all of its five members having begun individual trade and investment liberalization programs.[9] At a meeting in La Paz, Bolivia, the presidents of the five countries agreed to create an Andean common market by 1996. In a meeting in December 1991, the presidents agreed to more trade liberalization reforms in two days than had been agreed to in the previous 22 years of the Group's existence. The following were the agreements in this historic meeting:

- *Creation of a free trade area between Venezuela, Colombia, and Bolivia effective in January 1992*
- *Extension of the free trade area to Ecuador and Peru effective six months later in July 1992*
- *Establishment of a permitted list of exceptions to receive protection only until January 1993 (50 each for Venezuela, Colombia, and Bolivia; 100 each for Ecuador and Peru)*
- *Elimination of export subsidy programs for intra-Andean trade by January 1993*
- *Lower external tariffs to become a common external tariff in the context of a customs union by the end of 1994*
- *Creation of a provision detailing industrial, scientific, and technical cooperation between the member countries*

As a result of these measures, trade within the Group increased by 35% in both 1990 and 1991.

The Latine American debt crisis also had detrimental effects on the relatively successful CACM. As member countries erected non-tariff trade barriers to protect their foreign exchange positions, including multiple exchange rate schemes, the common external tariff ceased to be relevant. Then, in 1986, the Central American payments mechanism collapsed and each country was forced to individually undertake trade adjustments. The CACM was relaunched in 1993, this time including Panama, with objectives

---

[9] Chile elected not to participate in the relaunching of the Andean Group in 1990.

that were less geared to import substitution through explicit export promotion arrangements and a common external tariff between 5% and 20%, much lower than the previous level. These changes reflect a strong shift in focus — away from import substitution and protectionism — toward export-oriented policies.

Mercado Comun del Sur

MERCOSUR was created through the 1991 Southern Cone Common Market Treaty, also known as the Treaty of Asuncion. Its members are Argentina, Brazil, Paraguay, and Uruguay. This common market, based on reciprocity of rights and obligations between the members, involves:

- *The free movement of goods, services and factors of production between countries through the elimination of customs duties and non-tariff restrictions on the movement of goods, and any other equivalent measures.*
- *The establishment of a common external tariff, the adoption of a common trade policy in relation to third parties, and the co-ordination of positions in regional and international economic and commercial forums.*
- *The co-ordination of macroeconomic and sectoral policies between members in foreign trade, agriculture, industry, fiscal and monetary matters, foreign exchange and capital, services, customs, transport and communications, and other areas.*
- *The common market is based on the reciprocity of rights and obligations between members.*

MERCOSUR differs substantially from other recent agreements, such as NAFTA or the EU. MERCOSUR also represents a more ambitious undertaking since MERCOSUR's most developed member, Brazil, is still a relatively less developed country. Because of this distinction, MERCOSUR includes a specifically developmental function that is absent from other such integration movements. While MERCOSUR confronts questions about the exercise of state power as a development agent that may not occur with the same urgency in other parts of the globe, the issue is complicated even more because several MERCOSUR countries continue to struggle for macroeconomic stability.

In terms of **financial services**, the agreement that created MERCOSUR contained a requirement that the members commit themselves to continue advancing the process of harmonizing prudential regulations and consolidated oversight, as well the exchange of information on financial services.

Group of Three

Despite the geographic dispersion of the signatories, the 1991 Treaty on Free Trade defines trade relationships between Venezuela, Colombia, and Mexico. The agreement among the Group of Three contains the objectives to integrate economically through an elaborate set of principles and rules, including national treatment, most favored nation treatment, and transparency. The treaty is designed to:

- *Stimulate the expansion and diversification of trade among members.*
- *Eliminate barriers to trade and facilitate the movement of goods and service.*
- *Promote conditions of fair competition in trade.*
- *Increase substantially investment opportunities.*
- *Protect and enforce intellectual property rights.*
- *Establish the broad outlines for subsequent cooperation among members and in the regional and multilateral context.*
- *Create effective procedures for the implementation and application of the Treaty.*
- *Foster equitable relations while recognizing the differential treatments that result from the country categories established in LAIA.*

In the **financial services area**, Article 12 of the **Treaty on Free Trade** outlines the specific guidelines to which member countries are expected to adhere.

Article 12–08: Recognition and Harmonization

A Party may recognize the prudential measures of another Party (or of a non-Party) in the application of measures covered by Article 12. This recognition may be either accorded unilateerally, achieved through harmonization or other means, orbased upon an agreement with the other Party (or non-Party).

A Party according recognition of prudential measures under the above paragraph shall provide adequate opportunity to another Party to demonstrate circumstances exist in which thaere are, or would be, equivalent regulation, oversight, and implentation of regulations and, if appropriate, any procedures concerning the sharing of information between the involved Parties.

If the circumstances of both preceeding paragraphs are met, then the Party according recognition must provide adequate opportunity to another Party to negotiate accession to the agreement or to negotiate a comparable agreement.

Article 12–09: Exceptions

Nothing in this agreement shall be construed as means to prevent a Party from adopting or maintaining reasonable prudential reasons, such as: (1) the protection of investors, depositors, financial market participants, policy holders or claimants, or persons to whom fudiciary duty is owed by a financial institution or cross-border financial service provider; (2) the maintenance of the safety, soundness, integrity, or financial responsibility of finacial institutions or cross border financial service providers; and (3) actions taken ensuring the integrity and stability of a Party's financial system.

Article 12–10: Transparency

Each party shall make sure any measure it proposes to adopt regarding issues related to this chapter of the Treaty will be officially published or provided in other written form to all interested persons.

Article 12–11: Financial Services Committee

The Parties hereby establish the Financial Services Committee.

Article 12–12: Consultations

A Party may request consultations with another Party regarding any matter arising under the Treaty that affects financial services.

Article 12–19: Dispute Settlement

The Financial Services Committee shall establish and maintain a roster of up to 15 individuals who are willing and able to serve as arbitrators in controversies related to this article.

The Free Trade Area of the Americas

In April 1998, the leaders of 34 Western Hemisphere countries gathered in Santiago, Chile, for the Second Summit of the Americas. While the Summit agenda included such broad concerns as education, democracy, and poverty, issues related to economic integration dominated the meeting. In the summit's final declaration, the participating countries promised to create an historic Free Trade Area of the Americas (FTAA) linking all of the hemisphere's economies by the year 2005. Over the past few years, different countries in Latin America and the Caribbean have signed numerous trade and investment agreements. In addition to regional pacts, such as NAFTA, MERCOSUR, the Andean Pact, and the Caribbean Community (Caricom), there are bilateral agreements, such as the agreement between Chile and Mexico, as well as accords between regional groupings and individual countries. Even more significant, especially in light of the U.S. preference that governments participate individually in the negotiating process, was an agreement reached in San José that specifies that countries are free to negotiate as blocs.

The Plan of Action and Capital Market Development

In Quebec, leaders also released a **Summit Declaration** and a comprehensive **Plan of Action** to promote sustainable development; eradicate poverty, ensure peace and security, combat migration, promote human rights, including gender rights, fight drug-trafficking, increase internet connectivity and increase civil society participation. With respect to the **financial services sector** and **capital movement**, the Plan of Action noted:

> "The availability of capital at competitive rates is essential to finance private sector investment — a vital ingredient in economic development. Developing, liberalizing and integrating financial

markets domestically and internationally, increasing transparency, and establishing sound, comparable supervision and regulation of banking and securities markets will help to reduce the cost of capital by enhancing investor and depositor confidence."

Governments will:

- Form a Committee on Hemispheric Financial Issues to examine steps to promote the liberalization of capital movements and the progressive integration of capital markets, including, if deemed appropriate, the negotiation of common guidelines on capital movements that would provide for their progressive liberalization.
- Prepare, in cooperation with the **Inter-American Development Bank**, a comprehensive list of national capital regulations in order to promote transparency and support the discussions in the Committee on Hemispheric Financial Issues.
- Support the cooperative endeavors of the Association of Latin American and Caribbean Bank Supervisors and the Council of Securities Regulators of the Americas to provide sound supervision and regulation that support the development and progressive integration of markets.

The **Committee on Hemispheric Financial Issues** should also review problems of debt in the Hemisphere, taking account of ongoing work and drawing, as appropriate, on a broad range of expertise.

Tax Issues Guidelines on Capital Movements

The rapidly changing tax legislation of Latin America can complicate the planning of tax directors and businesses operating in the region. However, it appears that most countries in the region are adopting a uniform approach. Currency devaluation, export difficulties, and natural disasters have all taken their toll over the past few years. Nevertheless, the major Latin American Integration Association (LAIA) countries have shown signs of economic progress. According to World Trade Organization (WTO) statistics, foreign direct investment into Latin America increased significantly in 1997, to some extent at the expense of Asia, and although it faltered slightly in 1998 and 1999, the long-term investment interests have been maintained. The deregulation of Latin American economies has played a significant part in attracting multinationals to the region. As a result of a greater inflow of foreign investment, the individual nations' desire to protect their tax bases has been reflected in the development of international tax regimes that are similar to western policies.

Transparency of National Capital Regulations for Financial Services Firms

At the recent **Americas Business Forum (ABF)** in Buenos Aires, on April 5–7, 2001, the private sector made transparency a priority issue. As a result, the trade ministers agreed to take several important steps to increase transparency in the FTAA process. They agreed to make public the preliminary draft FTAA negotiating text. They instructed the **Committee on the Participation of Civil Society** to transmit submissions directly to the relevant FTAA negotiating groups, increase communication with civil society, including posting more information on the official web site and submit to the Trade Negotiations Committee a list of options to foster greater transparency in the FTAA process at the national level.

In addition to calls for transparency in the FTAA process, the private sector participants in the ABF workshops on procurement, investment and services also called for more transparent laws, rules and processes.

In September 2001, in response to demands to make the trade negotiation process more transparent and accessible, the U.S. Trade Representative (USTR) requested public comments on the draft text of the Free Trade Area of the Americas agreement. The National League of Cities focused its comments to the USTR on the proposed government procurement, investment, subsidies and services chapters.

Role of the United States in Leadership

It has been suggested that, without **fast track authority**, trading partners will understandably question the US commitment to the FTAA talks and willingness to deepen regional trade relations. The United States accounts for about 75 percent of total economic output in the hemisphere. Thus, the credibility of the hemispheric negotiations can be damaged if the resolve of the United States is not clear and emphatic. In the absence of clear signals from the United States, there might occur a **protectionist** backlash against the reform policies introduced in Latin America during the past decade — making it more difficult for Latin American countries to maintain and extend the liberalization already implemented.

Most countries in the hemisphere continue to pursue bilateral and regional free trade pacts without the United States. In most instances, the new agreements are designed as way stations to an eventual FTAA. However, the tariff preferences are accorded only to member countries and thus discriminate against U.S.-based exporters. Both Mexico and Canada have concluded free trade pacts with Chile; Mexico also has agreements with Costa Rica, Colombia, and Venezuela, and is talking with other Central and South American countries about similar arrangements. In addition, the MERCOSUR is solidifying its customs union and has entered into or is negotiating free trade "association" arrangements with Chile, Bolivia, and countries in the Andean Community.

References

Anonymous. (2001). The Americas: Small, vulnerable — and disunited; Central America. *The Economist (London),* 360(8234), 28.

Anonymous. (2000). Trade law passes for Caribbean and Africa: Will China be next? *Apparel Industry Magazine,* 61(6), 8.

Anonymous. (1999). The Andean region: A vision of integration. *Apparel Industry Magazine,* 60(9), SS22–SS27.

Blaine, M. J. (2000). Policy responses to capital inflows: Lessons from Mexico. *International Journal of Public Administration,* 23(5–8), 907–939.

Chen, I. (2001). Mexico's maquiladoras go way south of the border. *Global Finance,* 15(2), 71–72.

Cunningham, S. (2001). Identifying the common denominator. *International Tax Review (London),* 12(1), 19–23.

Dosal, P. (1999). Recent developments in Central American studies: A review of trends and prospects. *Latin American Research Review,* 34(3), 225–240.

Hazera, A. (2000). Recent trends in the evolution of Mexican financial groups. *International Journal of Public Administration*, 23(5–8), 1007–1034.

Lee, S. (2000). Globalization and the global city: Meeting the challenges of the twenty-first century. *East Asia: An International Quarterly*, 18(2), 18–35.

Mansfield, E. D. (2000). Trade blocs, trade flows, and international conflict. *International Organization (Cambridge)*, 54(4), 775–808.

Oriez, C. (1999). The European Union's data transport privacy regulations and safe harbor. *Information Executive*, 3(6/7), 1 & 8+.

Richards, D. G. (2000). MERCOSSUR: Regional integration, world markets. *Journal of Interamerican Studies and World Affairs*, 42(1), 159–163.

Schwartz, B. M. (1999). Customs compliance review. *Transportation & Distribution*, 40(12), 73–76.

Smith, J. M. (2000). The politics of dispute settlement design: Explaining legalism in regional trade pacts. *International Organization (Cambridge)*, 54(1), 137–180.

Tilson, D. J. (2001). Marketing the Americas: A vision for a new world union. *International Journal of Commerce & Management*, 11(1), 34–35.

Vamvakidis, A. (1999). Regional trade agreements or broad liberalization: Which path leads to faster growth? *International Monetary Fund. Staff Papers - International Monetary Fund*, 46(1), 42–68.

Weeks, J. (1999). Trade liberalisation, market deregulation and agricultural performance in Central America. *The Journal of Development Studies (London)*, 35(5), 48–75.

Chapter 6

Beyond Trade Agreements: European Monetary Union

Introduction

The **European Union (EU)** binds together the economies of the member countries in a "Single European Market." The goal is to create a seamless economy through which goods, services, capital, and people may flow freely. In order to achieve this goal, the EU has introduced single currency, replacing the individual national currencies. Furthermore, monetary policy of the EU is coordinated through a European **central bank**.

European Monetary Union: The Ultimate Cross-Border Agreement

In this environment, the operating rules for financial services have changed dramatically. A single license in one of the EU members now enables a financial firm to establish a presence throughout the EU. Regulatory guidelines have been harmonized through directives concerning banking services and capital adequacy. While this transformation has met with obstacles, neither problems with implementing directives, nor chaos in the currency markets, not even economic recession has stopped the forward momentum of the evolving financial market in Europe.

Origins and Membership

Treaty of Rome

The integration of Europe began in 1957 when six countries signed the **Treaty of Rome** — Belgium, France, Italy, Luxembourg, the Netherlands, and (West) Germany. As a result, the European Atomic Energy Community (EAC) and the **European Economic Community (EEC)** were formed. The goals of the EEC were to:

- *Lay the foundation for a closer union among the member countries.*
- *Form a common market by removing trade barriers.*
- *Work toward the continual improvement of living and working conditions in the member countries.*

In 1965, both the EAC and the EEC merged with the European Coal and Steel Community[10] to form the European Community (EC). In 1973, Denmark, the Irish Republic, and the United Kingdom joined the EC. Greece became a member in 1981, Portugal and Spain in 1986. Austria, Finland, and Sweden joined in 1995.

The European Union

Before 1985, the integration of Europe was to be effected through the harmonization of national rules and regulations. This meant that each EC member was to adopt identical rules and regulations — a difficult process at best. To overcome the difficulty, the EC Commission issued proposals in 1985 in a document entitled *Completing the Internal Market: White Paper from the Commission to the European Council.*[11] The 1985 White Paper recommended that the concept of **harmonization** be replaced, in many cases, with the concept of **mutual recognition**. Under mutual recognition, it is not necessary for each member country to adopt exactly the same rules and regulations. Instead, each member country is required to recognize the

---

[10] The European Coal and Steel Community was created by the Treaty of Paris in 1951 with the goal of transferring control of the materials of war from national governments to multilateral institutions. The founding countries were the six that signed the Treaty of Rome.
[11] A white paper is a document that presents a detailed and well-argued policy for discussion and political decision.

validity of the rules and regulations of other member countries. Of course, over time, the assumption is that mutual recognition would lead to the convergence of regulatory structures, that is, harmonization. The 1985 White Paper contained a list of 300 (later reduced to 279) specific measures for implementing general principles. In 1986, the Single European Act was enacted to implement the White Paper recommendations. This act created the Single European Market, effective January 1, 1992.

In February 1992, the EC Ministers met in Maastricht (the Netherlands) and signed a treaty (the Maastricht Treaty) that expanded the powers to the European Parliament, allowed the European Community to form common foreign and defense policies for the first time, and formed the European Union. The formation of the EU through treaties and directives has had a profound effect on the operation of financial markets.

Administration of the European Union

Coordination of EU policies and practices is centered in Brussels, Belgium. There are four main EU institutions:

The European Commission

The **European Commission** (1) proposes Community policy and legislation for the Council to consider, (2) implements the decisions of the Council of Ministers, (3) supervises the day-to-day implementation of EU policies, and (4) ensures that EU members comply with EC rules. The Commission is divided into 22 Directorates-General (DGs), each with a Commissioner that is responsible for its work. Some of the key DGs are:

- *External Relations*
- *Internal Market and Industrial Affairs*
- *Competition*
- *Employment, Social Affairs, Education*
- *Agriculture*
- *Transport*
- *Environment, Consumer Protection, and Nuclear Safety*
- *Science, Research, and Development*
- *Telecommunications, Information Industries, And Innovation*
- *Financial Institutions and Company Law*

- *Energy*
- *Customs Union*
- *Indirect Taxation*

The European Council

The **European Council** is the decision making body, adopting legislation on the basis of proposals from the Commission. Over time, Councils have evolved in particular policy areas including Agriculture, Finance, Industry, Research, Internal Market, Budget, Environment, Labor, and Social Affairs. Ministers attend councils from member countries and by representatives from the Commission.

The European Parliament

The **European Parliament** is directly elected by EC countries and is composed of more than 500 members. According to EU treaties, the formal opinion of the Parliament is required on many proposals before adoption by the Council. Typically, proposals are subject to the "Cooperation procedure." This involves the Parliament giving a first opinion when the Commission makes a proposal and a second opinion after the Council has reached a decision in principle.

The European Court of Justice

The **Court of Justice** rules on the interpretation and implementation of EU laws. The Court includes judges with representation from each EU country. Decisions by the Court are binding in each EU country and take priority over national laws.

There are several forms of legislation that are enacted by the EC institutions. **Regulations** have general application in all EU countries, need not be confirmed by national parliaments to be legally binding, and supersede national law. **Directives** are also binding on EU countries, but allow national governments to determine the method of implementation. **Decisions** are binding on those to whom they are addressed — EU countries, companies, or individuals — and enforceable in national courts. **Recommendations and opinions** have no binding effect, but merely indicate the view of the institution that issues them.

Banking Directives and the Single Passport

The **First Banking Directive on Coordination of Credit Institutions (1977)** was the beginning of Union-wide standards for banks. In this directive, "credit institutions" are defined as any firms that receive deposits or other repayable funds from the public and that grant credits for their own accounts. The First Banking Directive confers the right to establish a credit institution, suggests various financial ratios for such firms, and encourages the supervision of institutions (that operate in several European countries) through cooperative efforts among EU members.

The **Consolidated Supervision Directive of 1983** addresses the question of supervision of credit institutions across national borders within the EU. It stipulates that when one institution owns more than 25% of another, the two institutions shall be supervised on a consolidated basis. The supervisor of such institutions must review the accounts, exposure, and management of the consolidated institution at least on a yearly basis.

The 1985 White Paper also contained recommendations for the integration of financial markets. Three fundamental suggestions emerged:

- *Harmonization of the essential standards for (1) supervision of financial institutions and (2) protection for investors, depositors, and consumers*
- *Mutual recognition of laws and regulations beyond those necessary for essential harmonization*
- *Home country control and supervision for EU financial institutions that operate in more than one EU country*

The **Second Banking Directive on Coordination of Credit Institutions** addressed these issues and created the **single banking license**, or **single passport**. This directive, adopted in 1989 and effective January 1, 1993, builds on the First Banking Directive and the Consolidated Supervision Directive. With a license issued in any one of the EU countries, a bank may operate throughout the EU. The activities in which a bank may engage include deposit-taking, lending, money transmission services, leasing, participation in securities issues, issuing credit cards, travelers' checks and other means of payment, securities trading, foreign exchange trading, and portfolio management and advice. If the home country of a credit institution permits these activities, the credit institution may provide these services throughout the EU.

The two limits stipulated with respect to acquiring non-financial businesses are that (1) a credit institution may not hold a stake in a non-financial business that exceeds 10 percent of its capital and (2) the total value of all such stakes may not exceed 50% of capital.

In order for a credit institution from outside the EU to obtain a single passport into the EU, that firm must own or establish a subsidiary in one of the EU countries. Foreign institutions with subsidiaries that were established before the Second Banking Directive are grandfathered and may enjoy the full benefits of the single passport. It is also possible for a bank from a non-EU country to maintain only a branch in one of the EU members. However, such a branch will not enjoy the privileges of the single passport.

The Second Banking Directive also establishes the minimum capital required to establish a credit institution. A parent institution must have a capital base of at least $US6 million (approximately). However, once a parent has been established in one of the EU countries, it may branch into the other EU countries with no additional capital investment required.

The **Own Funds Directive** defines capital for credit institutions. The **Solvency Ratios Directive** incorporates the definition of capital into a minimum ratio that all credit institutions must attain. In conformity with Basle capital standards, the minimum ratio of capital to risk-weighted assets is 8%.

European Monetary System and the Exchange Rate Mechanism

After the World War II, countries with market economies adopted the Bretton Woods system (1944) in an effort to pave the way for international monetary stability and establish the U.S. dollar as the benchmark currency.[12] Assuming that this stability would continue, those who drafted the Treaty of Rome did not include provisions on genuine monetary cooperation. When the system started to show signs of weakness at the end of the 1960's, turbulence in the market led to the devaluation of the French franc (depreciation) and the revaluation of the German mark (appreciation).

---

[12] A direct result of this conference was the creation of the International Monetary Fund IMF) and the International Bank for Reconstruction and Development (the World Bank). Under this system, fixed exchange rates existed until the 1970s.

Because of these changes, the stability of the other currencies was threatened, as well as the system of common prices set up under the Common Agricultural Policy.

In response, at the summit in The Hague in December 1969, several Heads of State and Government decided to make economic and monetary union (EMU) an official goal of European integration. Pierre Werner, then Prime Minister of Luxembourg, was given the task of drawing up a report on how this goal might be reached by 1980. The Werner group submitted its final report in October 1970. In March 1971, while not agreeing on some of the key recommendations, the original members gave their approval in principle to the introduction of EMU.

In 1979, the **European Monetary System (EMS)** was established through a resolution of the European Council. The objective was to create a zone of increasing monetary stability within Europe. There were four main results:

- *The **European Currency Unit (ECU)** was created. The ECU is a GNP-weighted basket of member currencies, whose composition may change. Under the guidelines of the EMS, the composition of the ECU is subject to change every 5 years, or upon request, should the weight of any currency change by 25% or more.*
- *Short- and medium-term credit facilities were established for the members.*
- *Member countries agreed to maintain exchange rates within a band to be defined in terms of ECUs. The divergence indicator, a warning signal, triggered action on the part of the EMS Council and the member country whose currency was involved. Presumably, members would intervene in the foreign exchange market to correct this divergence. This new arrangement is called the **Exchange Rate Mechanism (ERM)**. Not all EU Members were members of the ERM, even though they are members of the EMS.*
- *The European Monetary Cooperation Fund was established to issue ECUs against member country deposits of gold and foreign exchange.*

The ECU served several functions — including the unit of account for the system and the basis for the divergence indicator. The ECU was first used to denominate and settle central bank debts and claims of member countries. In the fall of 1989, Luxembourg became the first EU country to encourage use of the ECU in everyday transactions. Soon private citizens were buying travelers' checks in ECUs, maintaining bank accounts in ECUs, purchasing Based-based mutual fund shares, obtaining ECU loans and mortgages, and making credit card purchases denominated in ECUs.

Members of the ERM agreed to correct the exchange rate variation of their respective currencies whenever the divergence indicator is activated. This means that ERM members were obligated to intervene in currency markets in unlimited amounts to bring their currency values back in line. To help accommodate any needed intervention of this nature, a short-term credit facility was initiated. Any ERM member required to enter the market in order to bring its currency value back within limits was given automatic and unlimited access to this facility.

In 1988, the Hanover European Council was asked to study the process of creating a unified European currency. The resulting **Delors Committee Report**, accepted in 1989, recommended that conversion to a totally unified currency take place in three stages:

- *Stage 1: A period of closer coordination and full participation of EC members in the Exchange Rate Mechanism.*
- *Stage 2: A transition phase during which (a) the central banks (monetary authorities) of EC countries would more closely coordinate monetary policy and (b) the framework for a European central bank, the Eurofed, would be established.*
- *Stage 3: The final point when the Eurofed assumes full control of European monetary policy and a single European currency circulates in lieu of existing national currencies.*

The Euro

The Plan for Convergence

A green paper published by the European Commission at the end of May 1995 contained a blueprint for a single European currency.[13] The program outlined by the Commission consisted of three phases:

- *The decision to launch the single currency and the identification of those countries qualified to use it*

---

[13] A green paper is a document designed to stimulate discussion on a particular topic.

- *The "irrevocable" fixing, within a deadline of the following 12 months*
- *Within three years of the second phase, transition to the single currency, with coins and notes introduced over a few weeks, at the most*

In December 1995, the EU heads of government met in Madrid, reaffirming January 1, 1999 as commencement of European Monetary Union. In addition, the other elements of the monetary union timetable were endorsed. The phase-in of the single currency was slated for the period between 1999 and 2002.

The EU heads of government decided that the name of the new currency would be the **Euro**. Those countries that are members of the monetary union beginning in January 1996 were asked to issue their tradable, government debt in Euros to create a reasonably large pool of financial instruments denominated in the new currency. Non-tradeable debt could continue to be denominated in the national currency during the transition period. It was not decided whether existing government debt would be converted into Euros. Commercial banks had the option of accepting deposits and opening transactions accounts in the new currency prior to the mandatory changeover date of January 2002.

Members of European Monetary Union

The European System of Central Banks and the European Central Bank assumed their full powers under Monetary Union, or Stage 3, and are responsible for issuing and managing the single currency that has replaced the national currencies. The United Kingdom, Denmark, and Sweden elected not to converge on January 1, 1999, that is, did not automatically join Stage 3. Greece joined the monetary union on January 1, 2001. The twelve converging countries on January 1, 2002 were Austria, Belgium, Finland, France, Germany, Greece, Ireland, Italy, Luxembourg and the Netherlands, Portugal, and Spain.

Criteria for Monetary Union

In order to join Stage 3, a member state must:
- *Achieve a high degree of price stability. The average one-year inflation rate before examination by EU authorities must not exceed*

*by more than 1.5 percentage points the inflation rate of the three best
performing EU members.*

• *Demonstrate sustainability of its government financial position. An
  excessive government deficit can disqualify an EU country from
  convergence. Public deficits may not exceed 3% of GDP, while total
  public debt may not exceed 60% of GDP.*

• *Observe the normal fluctuation margins provided by the Exchange
  Rate Mechanism for at least two years without devaluing its currency
  against the currency of another EU member.*

• *Demonstrate adequate control of its interest rates. For one year prior
  to examination by EU authorities, the long-term government bond (or
  comparable) interest rate may not exceed by more than 2 percentage
  points the long-term government bond rate of the three best
  performing EU members.*

These criteria have been established for joining Stage 3 of monetary
union, but one could argue that the criteria are desirable goals in a national
policy making context. Domestic price stability, adequate control of
government finance, proper management of the external value of domestic
currency, and a reasonable interest rate environment are conditions in any
event for which every sovereign state strives.

Impact on European Financial Markets

Early indications are that EMU is facilitating the efficiency of European
financial markets via several avenues. **Services charges of banks** in the
Euro-zone will be made more consistent under a plan developed by the
European Banking Federation. The plan is slated to begin July 1, 2002 and
to be completed by 2006. Under the plan, cross-border bank transfers will
cost no more than domestic transfers. **European government bonds** now
trade as a single asset class. Much of the previous price volatility in this
market has been eliminated because currency risk has been removed. In
2002, the Euro-zone government bond market was **1.5** times the size of the
U.S. Treasury securities market. From an admittedly small base, **corporate
debt** denominated in Euros **increased more than six-fold** between 1999
and 2000. **Liquidity** has been much enhanced. In 1999, the markets could
absorb an issue of no more than 500 million Euros. By 2002, an issue of 1.5
billion Euros was easily absorbed.

Discussions are underway to create a single regulator for the Euro-zone. Understandably, there is resistance to this idea, as national regulators must contemplate corresponding loss in regulatory power. Nevertheless, current estimates are that significant strides will be made in this area by 2007.

References

Anonymous. (2000). UK EMU entry: The economic, logistical and political hurdles and constraints. *Barclays Economic Review* (London), (2nd quarter), 2–8.

Anonymous. (2001). The future of globalization of the financial services industry. *Journal of Taxation of Financial Institutions*, 14 (3), 27 & 34.

Anonymous. (2001). Europe: Questions, at last. *The Economist* (London), 359(8223), 48.

Anonymous. (2001). Financial issues. *European Policy Analyst* (London), (3rd quarter), 111–124.

Anonymous. (2001). Leaders: A matter of priorities. *The Economist* (London), 359(8223), 10–11.

Bailes, A. (1999). European defence: What are the 'convergence criteria'? *RUSI* (Royal United Services Institute for Defense Studies) *Journal* (London), 144(3), 60–65.

Barnard, B. (1999). European investment bank. *Europe*, (383), 12.

Cooper, H. (1999). Europe unites: The launch of the Euro — What you need to know. *Wall Street Journal* (Eastern Edition), A5.

Dixit, A. (2001). Games of monetary and fiscal interactions in the EMU. *European Economic Review* (Amsterdam), 45(4–6), 589–613.

Kelsey, C. (2000). The shape of financial services in Europe. *LIMRA's marketFacts*, 19(3), 12–14.

Laidi, A. (2001). Euro: From financial markets to people's pockets. *Futures* (Cedar Falls), 30(11), 31.

Walter, N. (2001). How is the euro working? *Europe*, (404), 6–7.

Young, A. R. (2000). The adaptation of European foreign economic policy: From Rome to Seattle. *Journal of Common Market Studies* (Oxford), 38(1), 93–116.

Index